Carli Jay was just an average girl in her late 20s working a full-time job and living life to the maximum, partying and travelling the world, enjoying one day to the next. Although she had been morbidly obese her entire life and always struggled with her relationship with food, the latest diet trends, fads and exercise (or lack of…), she didn't let this stop her.

It wasn't until one day she had a rude awakening to her health that she decided to change all that and take control of not just her body but her health too. She wanted to change her whole lifestyle and her mentality towards being 'fit'.

Carli decided to make it her mission to prove to anyone no matter if it's 10 lb or 50 lb you want to lose, you really can do it! And all you need is you and just a little inner self-belief to make it happen!

FOLLOW ME ON SOCIAL MEDIA

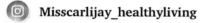 Misscarlijay_healthyliving

 Misscarlijay

Miss Carli Jay

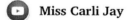 Misscarlijay

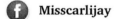 Misscarlijay

www.misscarlijay.com

This book is dedicated to every young girl, teen or woman who has ever been overweight in their life. To the ladies who have struggled with weight issues, tried all the whacky fads possible and are still in a constant battle with themselves over their body and weight. This, my lovelies, is for you.

Carli Jay

HALF THE SIZE, BUT TWICE THE LIFE

AUSTIN MACAULEY PUBLISHERS™

LONDON • CAMBRIDGE • NEW YORK • SHARJAH

A CIP catalogue record for this title is available from the British Library.

ISBN 9781528915519 (Paperback)
ISBN 9781528915526 (Hardback)
ISBN 9781528915533 (Kindle e-book)
ISBN 9781528961264 (ePub e-book)

www.austinmacauley.com

First Published (2019)
Austin Macauley Publishers Ltd
25 Canada Square
Canary Wharf
London
E14 5LQ

Prelude

As I sat at breakfast in this beautiful, all-inclusive resort on the coast of Mexico, I watched some of the guests shoving their faces with the unlimited amounts of food available in the all-inclusive buffet; I'd never seen anything quite like it.

I stared at an overweight family of 3, really noticing how big the 9- or 10-year-old boy looked for his age, devouring a plate of jam-filled donuts, custard-filled pastries and cream-covered cakes, and as he did so, I could feel my facial expression turn in to one of disgust, repulsed at all the calories, the fat and sugars in that amount of food, all just for breakfast... Not so much judging their choices, I was repulsed at my own choices. It was like looking in the mirror, as I remembered I too was eating donuts yesterday, downing them as if they were tic-tacs. Considering my own size, seeing others eating so much crap for breakfast almost made me reconsider my breakfast...almost.

Trying not to be hypocritical of their food choices, I looked down at my ever-growing stomach to which I looked like I was 22 months pregnant and having triplets any day now. But then again, I was on holiday. 'Enjoy yourself', 'Relax', 'We've paid for it', I could hear in my head as I picked at the pastry on my plate surrounded by eggs, bacon, fruit, yogurt, bread, biscuits and hash browns...

This holiday was a major turning point for me in the thought process to do something about my health and weight. As I got ready that morning after my big breakfast realisation, I decided to step on the scales in the bathroom and was beyond shocked to see 127 kg... Yes, 127 kg! (280 lb). The last time I had weighed myself, I was 113 kg (250 lb), some 18 months earlier, and that was only when I had to be weighed during a routine doctor's appointment.

Although slightly shocked at the numbers on the scale, I think subconsciously I knew I was getting bigger and bigger, but it really didn't seem to bother me; you know life just went on as it does.

I was never self-conscious about my weight and size, hence why I was picking out a bikini for the beach that day at a size 24, verging on a UK size 26. I really didn't give a shit, honouring my usual care-free attitude. I lived a happy life, had a boyfriend, lots of friends, a good job and did what I pleased. I never had a problem finding clothes or wearing what I wanted as shops these days simply keep making more and more sizes.

It dawned on me that morning, as I walked along the beautiful beach and white sand in Mexico, letting the sun kiss my skin that I missed this active outdoor lifestyle I once lived growing up on the Northern Beaches of Sydney, Australia. Since moving to the United Kingdom in 2010, I realised how my life had changed in terms of activity and being indoors so much, either working 60-hour weeks as a recruiter, or sitting on the couch all weekend like a TV junkie watching hours of box sets back to back. Not that in Australia I was slim or anything, I had been big my entire life; obesity was the only thing I'd ever known, but I think I lived a more active lifestyle in a way purely because of the climate, and how us Aussie kids were embedded in to a culture of sports and being outdoors.

Arriving in the UK, I was a size 16–18 at 24 years of age, and now, 3 years on, I was having an 'Oh shit' moment in my mind! Without really acknowledging it as the years went by, I had gone up four dress sizes and probably around 36 kg (80 lb) since moving to the UK. Don't get me wrong, I had thought regularly about doing something about my weight and health but I thought I was always going to be a big person, so I didn't really ever think I would be slim or lose the weight, and just thinking about it was enough for me. Doing something about it was a whole different ball game.

Although this time, something was different. Subconsciously, this time I knew I had to do something (really come on now, Carli), more so for my health and life than for anything, and so I put a lot of thought in to how I would go about doing this…

Chapter 1
The Wake-Up Call

After returning home to Surrey, just outside London where we had lived, I was having post-holiday blues, and quickly fell back in to my normal life of routine and not-so-good habits (yep, all those lovely bad habits we all have!). Six months on post-holiday, and after all that thinking about my health and body, fast forward and it was now the very last day of February 2014. I woke up that very cold and rainy morning and as I opened my eyes, I realised I couldn't feel the entire right side of my body! I was paralysed! *What the fuck?!?* I mentally screamed to myself. I couldn't move! My entire right side was numb and tingling all over. At the shock of waking up to this, I was trying not to panic and rather bring some sense to my brain. I can't be paralysed. *What is going on?* I thought to myself...

Well, that's what I initially thought, that I was paralysed as I literally couldn't feel anything down my side that I'd been sleeping on. It was like the entire side of my body was dead! As the shock died down and I tried to roll on to my back, I started to feel an odd tingling sensation running down to my hip and thigh...and at this moment, I realised it was just pins and needles, and a slight overreaction there on my part. But thank God, I wasn't paralysed; it was just pins and needles, like some people get a dead arm when you sleep on it from lack of circulation. I literally had a dead side from sleeping on it all night long. My body's sheer size had actually cut off part of my circulation from lying on it in the same spot for too long. As I managed to muster up some energy and effort to roll over, all the blood rushed back down my body and that was it. That was my wakeup call—literally—waking up to that was the trigger I needed to do something, anything! To do something about my health, my body, my life and ultimately do something about me!

I realised at this point the most movement and increased circulation my cardio-vascular system had seen in years was the walk from my front door to the car each day, from the car into the office, up a flight of stairs and back again. The rest of my day involved sitting on the couch, sitting at my desk, sitting in the car or lying in bed. *My poor body,* I thought. It's like it was crying out to get moving!

So that's exactly what I decided to do. I mentally slapped myself right across the face and said, "That's it, girl, get the hell up and move. MOVE your goddamn body!" And so, I did... I vowed to move myself all the way to a healthier me!

Chapter 2
Taking the First Steps

I had in the past attempted many a times to do something about my health, weight and fitness, such as buying a bike from a local Tesco two years earlier, assembling it then moving it to the corner of the room to collect fancy dust and hold up clothes that no longer fitted my growing form that I couldn't be bothered to fold or put away. See, I did attempt many times over the years to do something about my health and life but it usually resulted in spending money on quick fads, magical pills, waist bands but not actually physically doing anything about it.

But this bike had a way of staring at me as I sat with my big butt firmly on the couch each night. So, after that big wakeup call, I dusted off the old exercise bike in my lounge room and rearranged the clothes, which surely felt like I'd already done some exercise...but nevertheless, I then went through my drawers of old clothes and looked for anything that resembled gym wear and found some crappy old shorts and a top, along with a pair of dusty old moccasins from the back of my closet. I put on my favourite TV show that I would usually watch from the comfort of my corner couch, but instead, sat on the bike!

Here we go, Carli, I thought to myself! Then off I went, cycling for around 15–20 minutes, followed by a quick post-exercise stretch and that was it. Voilà! I had started! Started the journey I yet didn't quite know where it would take me, but I'd done it. Started.

The bit everyone fears and thinks they need help or advice to do. Yep, I'd put one foot in front of the other and started! I remember feeling so happy, satisfied, and for the first time, I truly believed this was the last time I'd start, because this time, there was no giving up. My life and health really did depend on it.

To this day, I still remember that feeling of standing in my lounge room and literally feeling the endorphins running through me, that I had committed to change my life just by a quick spin on the brand-new unused bike.

This was the biggest and hardest step I could actually make. It sounds weird but the physical movement of getting off the couch, and moving a metre away to sit on my bike was the catalyst in my whole journey beginning. I probably really could have kept going that day, but that was enough. I felt good that I had made a start and didn't want to push it now. I think it was more the mental thoughts of making that start that did more for me than the 20 minutes did, but it was a start, and I was happy and proud I had finally done it.

I truly think I knew I had to do something in the back of my mind, that bit is easy. The thinking about doing something bit, but physically doing something about it, that's a different story for a lot of us. I didn't have the desire to do, I was happy, I loved food, I loved relaxing and doing as little as possible, and did I say

10

how much I loved food? I did, though, like the idea of thinking about getting healthy, exercising, making yummy foods, improving my health, being fit, working out. Yes, the idea of it. But thinking and doing are two very different things …it's like we want someone to do it for us, or make us do it. We all want the results with little effort until some sort of sign or trigger gives us the encouragement to actually get up and do it, once and for all! And by God, I had that all right!

For me, it was that morning wake-up call of pins and needles I'll always be oddly thankful for. As who knows what would have happened to my body and health if I had chosen to do nothing. When I get going or really get in to a hobby, I am truly someone that is like a bull in a china shop. Giving it 150%, and once I find something I am good at, I enjoy it even more. I remember the days at school doing certain sports like swimming, softball, netball, tennis, rowing; I actually really enjoyed them once I got in to it. It was more the first step that I believe was the hardest. You think you have to change everything in your life, exercise like a crazy woman, starve yourself to get results, but boy was I wrong, you don't need to go through any of these extremes.

I started to think about this logically and think about the things I enjoyed, the things that had not worked for me in the past, as trust me, I really had tried everything, not necessarily because I wanted to lose loads of weight but because I seemed to have this addiction to 'trying new things' like fad diets, shakes, pills, magical seeds… Hey, because they looked like they worked in the TV ads right (More on this later).

But I realised nope, nope, they did not work! All they do is waste your money and time, and make you feel like you can't lose weight. They literally do the opposite of what you actually want for yourself. So all these fads, detoxes or latest diet trends were not going to be on the agenda this time round.

I wanted to think about a goal I could set for myself. I would be 30 within 18 months and needed to get healthy and enjoy a better quality of life for the long-term. I knew my work was bleeding me dry of time so how could I make small changes and still get results? I had to do this sensibly, logically and for the long haul. I just had to do it the right way… At this point, I didn't quite know what I was capable of, yet, so what goal should I set myself? 15 kg, 25 kg, 40 kg to lose?

I did genuinely like eating good foods, healthy options, fruits and vegetables, but I knew I ate too huge of a portion of even healthy foods, along with snacks, biscuits, chips and packaged meals as well…so I made a list of everything I was eating in a week: a 7-day diary of everything, and I mean everything! If you want this to work, you have to be completely honest, lay it all on the table. Don't cheat yourself when you've barely just started.

The list consisted of everything, even the milk that went in to my tea or coffee, or that one or two squares of chocolate I shared at work with the girls. You have to write it all down for the week and calculate a daily average of calories that you intake. As I tallied up my totals and saw the average I was eating per day, I couldn't quite believe it. My weekly average ranged from 4,000–5,000 calories some days! Yes, that's right, up to 5,000 calories! Goddamn, girl! (almost twice the recommended intake for a grown man!)

I know it's going to seem obvious of where I was going wrong with my food intake list—yeah, 2,000–3,000 calories gone wrong—but it wasn't just as simple as suddenly eliminating 3,000 calories overnight and problem solved; for a life-long obese girl who would eat even more than that sometimes, if I took drastic measures, I would end up just binging or cheating myself, as my body was not used to such a dramatic drop in food intake, and I knew I would fall off the wagon soon enough. So, I decided not to take on drastic measures but instead, I was opting for the long, slow way, but I knew this would really work.

I started making small changes each day and then each week. Having slightly smaller portions of my main meals, using a smaller plate and trying not to always have seconds (or thirds, like I used to). I was taking note of the calories I was no longer consuming on a daily basis and trying to reduce this from an average of around 4,200 calories per day to about 3,800 to start with for the first couple of weeks, which I know might not seem like much, but that's the idea: to reduce the amounts slowly over the coming 6–8 weeks, till I was at around 2,200. So in essence, my body and appetite had time to get accustomed to this new smaller amount almost without even realising it.

I did this by going back to my original 7-day food diary, and next to each item, I either wrote if: A) I could have a smaller portion, B) Swap out an item in the dish for a healthier less calorific item, or C) eliminate it all together, if say for instance, it was an unnecessary snack I was just having for no goddamn reason at all, but simply because Carli could…

There were some nights I was having two desserts! Yes, two, like it was almost normal to do this! I loved cake and sweet items, but it was about changing my mind-set. I didn't need two just because they were in the fridge. Save one for tomorrow, I tried to teach myself. Be happy, I was at least still having one dessert on occasion. I was definitely one of those people that when you have something savoury, you need something sweet after, oh and then yeah, if I have something sweet, I need something savoury—LOL—yes, just a constant circle of eating: savoury-sweet-savoury-sweet!

I opted for swaps on anything I could to try to reduce the calories down, or eat foods with less fats and sugars. I was swapping things like sweet potato for white potato, brown rice, wheat pasta or spinach pasta instead of regular pasta or sugar-free yogurts or fat-free options instead of massive slices of cake or whole packets of biscuits. Literally changing out anything that was a better version than the previous. Maybe not the completely healthiest option on the shelf yet, just something slightly better than I was already having. I knew this would be a continuous journey over the months to come, slowly getting rid of the bad and replacing it with the good!

I was being conscious of even healthy food portions, such as nuts, fruit and yogurts, educating myself on fats, good and bad, carbs, fibre content, minerals etc…and making sure I wasn't having too much of one and not enough of another.

Once I had a good head-start on my food and had tried to control that down to a reasonable level for a grown woman, giving myself a realistic time scale of eight weeks, I then addressed the activity, or lack thereof, part of my life and realised for someone that had 'no time' to exercise or get out of the house, I was watching about 20 hours of TV during the week after work and about 10 hours on the weekends. Yes, at this point in my life, I wasn't really getting out much, guess you could say I was well and truly a TV junkie, with my eyes glued to the box set for about 30 hours a week in total!

Over the course of the coming eight weeks, I kept on with the home cycling, doing this almost every day as soon as I got home from work, avoiding my cosy seat of the couch until after I had finished my new routine workout. If I couldn't do it every day, I was at least exercising every second day, doing 20–25 minutes followed by stretching. The best bit was I was starting to feel the mental reward of doing this and looking forward to coming home each day, clock watching at my desk till I as allowed to leave, bursting out of the office. Over the course of those first couple of months, I steadily increased my activity from the 25 minutes every second day to gradually building up to doing 45 minutes pretty much every day, not forcing myself, simply because I was enjoying it and my body was starting to crave it more and more.

On the weekends, at times, I just kept pedalling, one day doing 90 minutes whilst watching two episodes of *Sons of Anarchy* back to back. The time just flew by, I couldn't believe it. This then carried on to most weekends, even one occasion I think I cycled for almost three hours watching some movies on a rainy Sunday morning. I know it seems long to some people, but I thought to myself, *Well, you're just going to sit on your butt and watch the movies, probably snacking on chips or biscuits like you used to do, so why not cycle away instead, minus the snacks!* It didn't have to be a crazy sweat-dripping marathon ride. I just leisurely cycled away keeping my limbs moving and circulation pumping away. Those pins and needles were such a distant memory for my body.

I knew whilst the TV was on, and by covering the bike clock with a towel, I could distract myself to keep exercising, as I was also really starting to enjoy it— like a true woman, multitasking and making the hours in a day work for me, enjoying two pastimes at once, making the most of my Sunday!

By the end of the first two months, I had lost 14 kg (30 lb)! I was ecstatic, I could seriously not believe it! What?! I could lose weight, lots of weight! I was NOT big-boned, I didn't have to be obese. That really was a state of mind I had always been told, so I lived that way, almost embracing my obesity—a little too much, looking back now.

Even though at 113 kg (250 lb) I was still on the larger side of life, I knew what I was doing was working once and for all. The results spoke for themselves, and I was doing it all by myself, that was the most exhilarating thing about it, which made me want to do it even more!

So from there on out, it became like a great new habit, a routine, a healthy cycle; the more I saw results, the more changes I made. The more changes I made, the more I saw results and from there, it really started to take off. I knew I was on the right path and with my bull-in-a-china-shop mentality, determination to prove I could do this and how I began to feel mentally and emotionally, there really was no stopping me! This long haul, logical way really was the only way for me!

That's when my overall goal finally came to me! I knew I could do this, whatever I set my mind to. So hey, why not go the full way and lose half my body weight. I didn't question if I could do it, more of a case of how-what-when I was going to do it? With that mind-set, working in tune with myself, I committed to myself and vowed for any person out there who believes they can't do it that I would! I would lose half my body weight, yep a whole 63.5 kg (140 lb). I wanted to do it in a realistic two years.

See, being realistic is key; I knew this was sure as hell not going to happen overnight! And the best bit of all, I wanted to do it all alone. Yep, just me, myself and I battling it out, spurring myself on. I was going to be the motivation I needed to reach my goal. No family support, no husband to come home to, no personal trainer, no diets, weird gimmicks or minus 1,000 calorie diets, no detoxes, no surgery or slimming pills—just little (big) old ME!

Chapter 3
Determination

As the days and weeks started to roll by in to my third month of my transformation, I looked in the mirror one day, and I had to double take. I couldn't believe my reflection! My face wasn't as puffy and round as the moon like it had been for so many years, and this was the first time I really noticed I was dropping those kilos! I think when we mentally picture ourselves, we picture how we 'think' we look to ourselves, or how we 'wished we look' to ourselves, and it's sometimes hard to see what you look like to someone else. What I saw that morning was real! I looked less bloated, my face was changing, cheek bones very faintly coming through, I think I even had a collar bone under there somewhere! So, I got out the camera and took some pictures in my underwear of my body and new size. Now, it wasn't a big difference, but hey, it was different OK, and that's what counts, any small difference is a change. I compared them to the pictures I had taken in Mexico the previous year, and I was amazed, and pleasantly surprised.

I had always been told body fat literally comes off in layers across the whole surface of the body, like pealing an onion; we hold the same body shape underneath, we just come in at every point on the body. Comparing the two sets of pictures really showed this. I still had the same shaped legs, arms, stomach, but I could see they were reducing in size. These pictures made me smile, squealing on the inside, I could see it all coming to a reality. Everything I was doing was working, and this spurred me on to keep at it! The proof was there, and I always kept reminding myself not 'you can do it', but 'you are doing it!'.

At that moment, I decided I was going to document my journey more for myself but also as proof. (Proof because I think subconsciously, I always knew one day I would share my story…)

Taking pictures for me at any size, lumps, bumps and all, was not a big deal, as I said I was never self-conscious at any size and I think this is really important to keep you motivated. No matter what journey you are on, what size you are, you need to see the hard work you are putting in as this will push you to keep going. Be your own motivation to succeed!

Throughout my journey, one thing people have always asked me is what kept me motivated? So, yes, as corny as it sounds, I did. I kept myself going every single day, through the great amazing days, the mediocre days and the tough days. Things like pictures remind you of where you have been, what you are now and where you are heading. You need to really look at these pictures and not criticise them, or say what you don't like about yourself, but really look at them and see what you love and all the areas of improvement you are conquering. Also, besides how you look, think how it's made you feel inside and out, and know everything you are doing is for a better you, for better health, a better fitness level, and of course a better quality of life!

To get to any goal in life people always say you need to measure your success along the way, and so that is exactly what I was doing. Measuring and assessing my steps to my goal. I put the pictures side by side on my laptop like I was in a Weightwatchers before and after advert like I used to see on the TV as a kid. I got so excited to think what my next photos would look like after another 10 kg gone, or 35 kg gone, and then I pictured what I could look like once I had lost that 63.5 kg (140 lb). In my head, I could see this nice svelte frame, curvy hips, flat stomach, slimmer arms, toned thighs and muscle definition I had never had and boy, oh, boy did I really like what I was visualising!

It was like a dream, but not just any dream this time, it was going to become a reality, I could feel it! I could really see it! I really started to believe in my own an ability, that I would finally do this once and for all. I knew I had made the start, and was on track, doing well, but hey, I'm only human and some days, the tiniest bit of doubt would try to creep in to my mind and I would think to myself, 'Am I doing this? Is this really my life?'

Because for so many years, almost three decades really, I had been told I would be big my entire life, that I was just big boned, or that it's hereditary, or that my dad's side of the family is all big so I will be too…but no, not this time! This time, I would be smaller, I would be slim, I would actually be the petite one for a change. I didn't have to just shop online in the plus size section anymore!

I was getting excited by the possibilities and this is where my mind really began to change! Why not, I thought, I've seen these weight loss TV shows, read magazine articles, books about health and the body, and the mind really is an amazing thing, it's not rocket science, I too can lose this body fat! That 63.5 kg target was in sight, half my body weight a whopping 10 stone, practically a whole person! (Really, could I do that? No, correction, Carli, you will do that!)

I battered away the little self-doubt that does come up every now and again and thought, *YES, you bloody well can do it, Carli, you can do anything you put your mind too! You always have and always will.*

****

Looking back over my life, I have been and always will be a very strong woman mentally! I think that has got to be one of my best qualities, to which I will be forever grateful for. A strong mentality is everything, it will see you though any situation you come across.

I have been through some tough situations in my own life, low points, setbacks and hit rock bottom…but one thing I can happily say is that I've always seen the positive in even the very worst of situations I've been in and had dealt to me in life. I am thankful for all the situations, good and bad, and take them as lessons and growing points. I've always taken care of myself, been independent and positive on my outlooks, going after what I believe in and anything I want to do. So, I truly believe when you want something bad enough, nothing should hold you back, just go for it! We will all be old and grey one day so, don't look back with regrets on anything! I really think you need to have this mentality with any goal or dream you tackle in life, including any body and fitness goal, it's the only way you are going to get there. Mind over matter and all that jazz as they say…does actually have some sense to it.

I know if you want something, don't wait for it to happen or be given to you. My mum always used to say to me, "If you want something done in life well then you better do it yourself, as then you know the job gets done…" and I think to this day, I still live by this.

So, with all my willpower, self-belief, pure dedication and all the inner self motivation I could muster up, I truly believed I was going to do this and I would not stop till I got to my goal.

I knew it would be tough, I knew there would be bad days and hurdles along the way, but under no circumstances would I give up this time, I knew I could do it. I had lost 13 kg already, more than I had ever lost in my entire life time, so what would stop me from going the full way.

At this point, I knew I was truly capable of what I set my mind too, the mind over matter concept is truly amazing, but you really need to channel in to it, zone in, focus! Not just say it, but be all about it. It's like channelling your inner soul and I know as corny as that sounds, if you can't do that or believe in it, then you won't get to your goal. The body will follow naturally what the mind believes.

It's odd that, in life, people often believe more in others than they do in themselves, but you have no control over others, yet you do over your own actions. So, I began to visualise everything I wanted: my life, my body, my perfect ideal weight for me, my surroundings, the clothes I would wear, everything I could do and have when I got to my goal, and I really liked what I saw. In fact, I absolutely loved it!

Visualisation is a very powerful tool to use alongside the handwork you are putting in for your goals. And they do say the more you visualise your life, and what you want, the universe does align it, and you have to really believe in this. What you want, you need to speak in to existence as if you already have it. See you and your body as you've always imaged it could be. What have you got to lose? Go on, try it and you might just get something you have been wishing for subconsciously your whole life…

Chapter 4
Let's Start from the Beginning: Childhood Days

People often ask me how I got to the size I was, in the first place, like how did I let it happen?? I had always been overweight since I was young, and I can always remember being the chubby kid in pre-school and kindergarten in Sydney, noticing I was bigger than the other kids in my class. But Mum always reassured me I'd grow in to it, or rather that I was just big boned…and not to worry as 'big was beautiful'! Bless her cotton socks!

So, from starting out like this, and learning early on that this is how I was and that it was okay to be overweight, I think I then became so accustomed to it. A lot of my family members were also overweight or above the average.

I think because of that mentality, a lot of my doubt to ever be slimmer along with all my bad habits stemmed from my childhood days. But by no means is this in any disregard to my mum or how she raised me or what she fed me. She was, and still is, the kindest and caring woman I know, and always just wanted us to enjoy life and our childhood as best we could. Also, to be fair to her, if me and my sister asked for a treat after school or snacks at home, even when she said, "No, girls, it will ruin your dinner." I'm pretty sure me and my sister had them anyways, we never heard no when it came to food.

Studies have shown that we do learn a lot from our surroundings and what we see from our parents, siblings, childhood friends, especially in early development and the first five or so years of our life. My parents were big foodies too, and they always cooked with fresh ingredients, good meats, fish, vegetables grains etc, and our cupboards and fridge were always stocked full of food, including fruit, snacks, biscuits, chocolate, ice creams, the full works!

There are many scenarios I could touch on from my childhood memories, but from as young as I can remember, this particular family dinner setting I'm going to recount always plays on my mind for some reason, and I think gets to the point of what I'm trying to get at when it comes to kids and their relationship with food from an early age. Scenarios as a child and their relationship with food can shape certain behaviours and habits for years to come, even though you may not realise it at the time. It sure did take me some time to realise all of this.

****

It was a standard evening in our household, dinner was usually set by 6 P.M., with my parents calling up to me and my sister in broken English-French: "A la table. Dinner is ready!"

I had a very strict father who always expected you to do as he said. I remember sitting around our table near the kitchen in our usual places with the TV playing on low in the background and being served up a massive plate of food. My parents always fed us portions the same as theirs, as if a 5-year-old needed the same amount of food as grown adults.

I remember my sister and I shovelling down the food before the delay of being full kicked in, mouthful after mouthful eating as much as we could. We would then ask to be excused from the table or say we had enough, but always knew we would be told to stay. "No, finish your plate before you can leave the table." And so we would literally force every bit of food in to our mouths, and as I write this, I still get chills thinking of this one particular memory in the back of my mind.

As I hear my father yelling 'Mange, mange' in his thick French accent at me as I procrastinate and start making a fuss, shoving the food around, protesting that "I can't eat anymore..." and as I write this, I can actually feel what I felt all those times at the dinner table, the feeling of my throat and mouth being so dry trying to chew every last morsel feeling so full like I would be sick, especially those awful green lentils my father used to cook that tasted horrendous in his stewed concoction of a meal he would make time and time again.

I remember one day, with tears welling up in my eyes, I was told that 'if I didn't finish my plate, I'd be in trouble'. So, I kept shovelling every mouthful in to my mouth, filled with resentment until one occasion when I spat out the last mouthful with rebellion, almost a regurgitation, as I really thought I was about to be sick all over my plate, and hoped that if I spat the mouthful out on my plate, he wouldn't make me eat the rest and see that I didn't need to finish my plate, that, in fact, I really had, had enough...

To this day I don't remember if he made me finish it... I think somehow, I blocked that bit out if he made me re-eat it or not.

I can still hear my mum's voice saying, "Oh, leave them alone, they're full." And her face full of pity always trying to reason with him and stick up for us, knowing full well he wouldn't listen as his rules were his rules; we had to finish our plates!

I hated lentils for my entire life because of this dish he made and scenario at dinner, and it wasn't until I was 31 that I decided to buy some, cook them my way, and eat them for the very first time since I was a child. And yes, I enjoyed them for once in my life, because it was my decision to have them along with how much I needed to eat...

So, the concept of feeling full was never fully understood with me as a child or only lasted momentarily. I think from a young age I had a big internal stomach and I could eat, eat, as I was conditioned to finish everything, always! "Don't waste food," my parents would say, "there are starving children in this world that would love that food!" Even when full, I would still eat and that sick-full feeling didn't even put me off anymore. I was like a bottomless pit, constantly chewing on something, anything! But now, even thinking about that overly full feeling makes me cringe and feel ill. I just hate it!

Despite eating healthy foods and lots of yummy fruit, veg, salmon, prawns, steak whilst growing up, I also loved snacking, especially whilst watching TV...(funny how that was my favourite past time as an adult too...)

I could have some toast or cereal for breakfast and a piece of fruit, sounds good, right…but then I could devour a whole tin of biscuits with my dad and sister dipping them in our morning coffee or hot milk, as this was something he did frequently especially on the weekends, sitting at the kitchen table reading his newspaper munching on biscuits for breakfast.

Shortly after that, I might feel like some cheese on toast or yogurt, or even ice cream, and mind you, it was probably only 10 A.M. on a Saturday morning and I am picturing myself about eight years old sitting there on the family couch watching *Agro's Cartoon Connection* or *Rage* music clips on the ABC.

We would then have a healthy lunch of salads, chicken, tuna pasta, garlic prawns etc…but by mid-afternoon, I would be back in the cupboard eating chips, snacks, roll-ups, cheese and biscuits, lollies etc…

Food habits, both good and bad, I do believe are adopted from a young age, as to what is put in front of you and what you're taught is how you build relationships and dependencies with food. I had become so used to snacking and constantly going to the cupboard for my next item to munch on, it's like I was on autopilot.

Usually on a Saturday and Sunday afternoon, instead of being out playing with friends, or my next-door neighbours, doing something active, (god forbid we do that and play like children) my father, being French and incredibly old school, would have a 'siesta' and also make me and my sister do so as well.

Looking back now, this thought makes me incredibly sad, I feel like I had wasted weekends and had hours deprived of my childhood where I couldn't just be a kid and enjoy playing like any other kid on the street would.

I remember once being round at my friend's house behind ours after lunch playing hide and seek, running around enjoying ourselves to suddenly hearing my name being yelled for over the back-yard fence, and summonsed that it was siesta time. My father being one for discipline and doing what he said, we knew we had to go.

I felt miserable so probably went and got something to eat too and then was forced to have these ridiculous afternoon naps for 1–2 hours mid-afternoon, even when we weren't tried, had barely used up any energy that day and probably had 3,000 calories already being converted to fat in our bodies.

We would then usually have dinner around 5:30/6 P.M., yes, early I know, and be told to be back in bed by 8 P.M., and if not, there were consequences.

Looking back now, there are so many signs there of everything you should not do with a child, force them to eat, over feed them, let them snack in between, deprive them of playing and using energy. But I feel my father had no concept of this or knew how to let children be children, and my mum, to an extent had no control over his decisions and rulings. He was not a man that knew reason or how to flex on his opinions and values.

Every weekend was like that for years to come, confined to food and sleep, and hence why I think ever since I was four or five years old, I can remember being the chubby kid, even in pre-school, then in to my primary school days, and in to my teen years, I knew I was bigger than my peers.

Although I knew some kids may have called me names, or behind my back I was made fun off, as children can be nasty without realising it in school. For some reason, and maybe luckily for me, it never really got to me. It's like I was beyond comfortable with being bigger than the 'normal' average kid, as that's what I was told I was big, chubby, like my relatives, hereditary…and so, I kept on day after day, eating, snacking and doing just a little activity if and when I was allowed or had to.

I remember in primary school when we had P.E classes or athletics carnivals, I would sometimes forget my gym kit on purpose or leave my sneakers behind, hopping then I wouldn't have to take part. I wasn't confident with running or really physical sports, mainly because I was never encouraged to do it at home, alongside not being very good and often coming last in raises, so I just tried to avoid doing it.

Although I have really fond memories of the school holidays and half term breaks, when my mum would often take my sister and I to our local ice rink, ice-skating for a few hours at a time. Despite not being amazing at it and holding on to the side for a few rounds avoiding looking like a baby giraffe stranded in the middle, I actually did really enjoy this, and always had fun, trying to get better and better each time.

The only other thing I actually really loved was swimming, as we did have a pool at home, and maybe as I could do that more often (when not sleeping or eating), and had an ounce of confidence in that, it was the one time I was free to be a child, diving in and out of the water, making up games and enjoying playing for once. Even taking part in the school carnivals on this one as I was remotely good at it!

Funny as to this day, these are two of my favourite sports and hobbies I often do in my leisure or for some me time!

Chapter 5
Adolescence

As I went on to high school in my teenage years, we were then 'forced' to do a Saturday sport. To me, I remember thinking it was forced as I wasn't used to being encouraged to play or move about, but to most other kids, they probably saw it as a fun activity. But to this day, I am so thankful that my school had this programme, as I got introduced to so many activities I didn't even know existed, or that I was actually good at, getting me out and about on the weekends more often.

I remember choosing softball and being really good at it and actually enjoying the sport, because of my big strong arms, I was one of the best batters and even got home runs pretty much every game. Then the next term, I tried netball and again I had so much fun, and found I was quite a natural, especially at goal shooter or goal attack, I was one of the top point scorers in my team.

As the years went on, throughout high school, I tried so many different activities, even despite my height and size I gave rowing a go! This was amazing to me, I thought it was something only the tall slimmer girls at school were good at. I was enjoying getting up at 4 A.M. to be on the water, rowing by 5 A.M., training before school started for the day, and after almost every day too. This was the first exposure I had to full on training, weights and even going to a local gym on occasion for added workouts. See, when I like something, I am almost over eager to do it! I remember having so much fun with our crew, competing at the regattas, even coming 3rd at the biggest race of the year when I was around 16.

At this point in my life, from all the activity I was doing and eating slightly better, my body was probably pleasantly shocked, burring more calories and moving my body than I ever had in my life. I remember losing a little bit of weight, but not that I really noticed at the time until one of my friends said it to me when we were down at Balmoral Beach one day during the summer holidays. But I don't think it really sank in at that age, or that I understood the changes that were going on with my body from the positive effects of so much sport. I just saw it more as a sport I was doing for one semester at school then that was it.

After the rowing season finished and school was over for the year, I remember not continuing to burn any calories but still eating a hell of a lot, as I had been to fuel my body for all the extra training it was doing. That massive shock to my system from the drop of 8–10 extra hours of physical activity each week, down to pretty much none again, I ballooned in Year 11 at school to my biggest yet! I was an adult size 16–18 and probably around 85 kg (187 lb) as a 17-year-old (what the average grown man can weigh). And from this day, I remember my weight going up and up over my last two years of high school until I was 18.

I remember noticing more and more stretch marks all over my body, my clothes getting so tight my mum had to buy me new school uniforms and even they were struggling to find me a size that fit, I had to get them specially ordered and custom made to fit my every growing size.

During my late teens, the girls and I from high school would often head to one of the many beaches near where we lived, meeting up with the guys from the local all-boys school we were friendly with. I was often just friends with these guys, as majority of the boys during their teenage years are accustomed to going for a skinnier girl, or the very pretty ones. I'm not going to beat around the bush here, teenage boys don't usually go for the fat girl. Although on the rare occasion, I did have a couple of boyfriends (they feel for my bubbly personality and charm!) You know those teenage relationships that we all have, last a couple of months, share a few kisses and dates, get annoyed when he doesn't text you back? Yeah, those ones, nothing to write love stories about. But I often found I was the girl best friend to the guys more often than not. But to be honest, I will always be thankful for those friendships and it actually did teach me a lot about guys, how they think and act. Some of whom I'm still friends with and they are like brothers to me to this day. Although, even in the present day, I sometimes do struggle to tell if a guy is actually interested in me, as I get along with guys well, and always assume they are just wanting to be friends. No joke LOL! I was never used to guys approaching me, but if they did, it was usually about my cute friend and them wanting me to put in a good word for them.

During our summer holidays, we would all head down to Balmoral Beach baths, a popular place for all the local schools to hang out, diving off the pier, swimming, working on our tans, attempting to flirt with the boys and having cheeky drinks and puffs on our first cigarettes and joints as you do at that age.

These were the times I really noticed how much bigger I was than my friends, especially as I was always in a one piece, slightly trying to hide how big I was getting, but also thinking to myself 'Oh, fuck it, they can see me anyways, who am I kidding', with my much slimmer friends in the latest bikinis. I could never really share clothes with my besties, like most girl groups do growing up borrowing each other's jeans or dresses. I was probably about five sizes bigger than they were. It's weird how these memories are the things I remember about my overweight teens. I guess as teenage girls, we are impressionable and want to fit in, but oddly enough, I got used to being the odd one that stood out, who wasn't always like the rest, and somehow, I managed to pull it off, along with my friends accepting me for who I was, no matter what size and loving me just how I was. I was always part of the popular group and never shying away from a group situation, parties or school dances. I really did make the most of my high school days, and looking back, those were some of the best days of my life where I learnt who I was, how people can treat you because of how you look and to never under estimate who you and what you can do. I learnt to just be me and let people like me for who I was or don't, I didn't care, I was happy being me. Take it or leave it.

****

Writing these childhood and teenage chapters, I knew would be odd for me as for anyone that knows me well or follows me knows I am a very positive person and I take everything in my stride, using it as a positive to push on forward, but I knew I had to write this part of my journey as I believe so much of my life to this day and thought process around weight, eating and exercise came from those very early years as a child and even my teenage days.

I had an awful relationship and understanding of food, that is was actually fuel for my body not boredom. The feeling of feeling full, nutrition, how to say no to food and discouraged from physical activity, but hey, at least I was getting plenty of hours sleep, right?!

Now, I am not at all putting all the blame on my parents, as entering adolescence and adulthood, I had my own brain and responsibility to take for my decisions, but to some degree, I think the damage had already been done and I had instilled so many bad habits that the thought of undoing them was more effort than it was worth to me, and I'd learnt to enjoy and embrace who I was.

But I do think it is so important to teach children a healthy relationship with food, nutritional values and of course, the importance of fun activities and exercise, but not in a forced way. It needs to be from a young age as we do remember a lot more than you think, and it's not till your adult life that you may realise some of these teachings that you absorbed, then moulds your later thought processes and actions.

These extracts and memories from my younger days are just a few recollections from when I was a child, which I think shaped my bad habits I kept in to adulthood. I could go in to a lot more detail but I think you get the idea, along with what I'm trying to address, and I hope this has started to answer the question of 'How did I let myself get to 127 kg (280 lb) at 28 years of age' before I did something about my every growing body size.

This all was just the beginning of what was to shape my decisions and habits for the next 20 years to come. And yes, people may say well, why didn't I do something about it at 18, 19, and so on, and to be frank, by then I was so used to how I was, doing what I wanted, eating what I wanted, in all honesty, I didn't care to.

By then I was so used to it, and owning who I was, I was confident with my body and it never held me back. After so many years of being told that's how I was, its hereditary or big boned, I was like 'Yeah, I'm big, I know it, and so what?' That was my attitude that I had on my size and it would stay that way, until something in the future could try and change it…

Me aged 2–3yrs

Me aged 5–6yrs

Me aged 10yrs, playing softball

Ready for School Formal, aged 15yrs

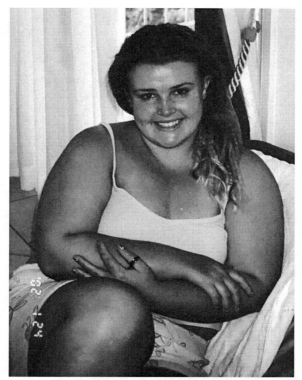

Me aged 15–16yrs

Me aged 14-15yrs, at school with my best friend, Emma

School rowing, aged 14–15yrs (me on the far right)

Mum and I, aged 16yrs

Me and my friend Jess at our school formal, aged 18yrs

Me and my friend, aged 18yrs

Chapter 6
Wild Child, Crazy and Free

As I left school, approaching my 20s, and went out in to the world of not having this set routine to eat breakfast, have morning tea, eat lunch, have afternoon tea, eat dinner etc...I actually lost some weight without even realising it.

I was having fun, eating when I wanted to, working, earning my own money and meeting new circles of friends, basically doing what most normal school leavers do after entering the big brave world after all those years of studying at school.

I was enjoying my last few years in my teens partying (a lot), shopping with friends, hanging at the beach as us Aussies loved to do and generally having a good time. From all the late nights out I was now enjoying, as not having school the next morning, my days also consisted sometimes of sleeping in till midday, mooching around till mid-afternoon having 'breakfast' and then going out all night with friends again.

We would be cruising the streets in our modified cars till the early hours of the morning, hanging out in the car scene, going to illegal street race meet ups and drag racing with groups from all over Sydney with done-up sports cars, Japanese racers, and V8s. It really was like a scene out of The Fast and the Furious. As well as the car scene, there were our weekly club nights on Thursday through to the early hours of Sunday morning at our local hangouts, drinking, dancing and yes, dabbling in recreational drugs.

I wasn't eating as regular or as much as I previously did with all those set meals, and instead, I was out dancing all night and pretty much on a liquid diet of cocktails and vodka cranberries drinking the night away with friends partying till the sun came up watching the sunrise over Newport Beach.

Drugs were always a massive part of the night life in Sydney during these years, and without fail, every week I would experiment with drugs such as speed, coke and pills as they were so readily available and I guess at that age, I was curious to try things and 'have fun'.

During this period from the lack of physical calories I was taking in compared to my school days, not being in this set routine with meals, and actually being out more doing activities, I did see some weight come off, but this wasn't necessarily a good thing the way I was going about it, even though it was unintentional. I wasn't trying to lose weight, but the effect of drugs and alcohol, almost like an appetite suppressant, I had dropped a few kilos without even knowing it until my clothes were feeling looser. I remember one day popping on a denim skirt, pulling it up and fastening the zip, before the skirt fell down my hips and sat on my thighs.

"Wow, that's a first," I giggled to myself, and I can't deny I was slightly happy, but also a little shocked.

If you've followed me on Instagram or seen some of my interviews on YouTube, I've never hidden this fact about me or my wild child crazy partying ways. It was part of my life, and I am as raw and as real as they come so I am going to talk about this subject openly, as I'm sure it would all come out eventually. But before I begin, sorry, Mum! Although I'm sure you had your suspicions back then!

I started smoking cigarettes from my early teens, or attempting to, I had tried weed by the time I was 14 and experimented with softer drugs before the age of 18. But it wasn't until I was about 19 and through till I was 23 years old that I started taking speed quite regularly to aid in my partying ways. I drank a bit but wasn't overly wowed by that or the feeling of being drunk and I preferred to take speed rather than drink endlessly to get wasted. We would go out clubbing all hours of the night usually 3–4 nights in a row then party during the day at a friend's house, continuing on the all-night benders, pool parties, BBQs and generally having a great time.

Don't get me wrong, these were some fun memories, and I can't lie, some amazing nights out, even though they may or may not have been drug fuelled, but I guess days like these are part of most teen's or 20's experimental days. The people that knew me from those days and hung out with me on many occasions will know what I mean when I say we partied hard and really made the most of those days when you feel you're young and care free with little to no responsibility!

But even then, I was still bigger than most of my friends those days and on the chubbier side of life. So, if you think drugs and partying may help your waist line, they don't—and it wasn't till after I stopped that I really felt the effects of what these drugs can do to your system and had done to mine. Hence why I decided to talk about this part of my life and be honest with my experiences.

As I had always been big, my body and skin was droopy and as my weight went up and down from the drugs and party, I'm sure I looked malnourished, along with the really poor skin and acne I had on my face and all the way down my neck, weak dry hair and my overall nutrition was suffering.

Throughout my partying days in 2009 and early 2010, I was working as a freelance Beauty Therapist and Masseuse after recently finishing my studies in this field. From learning all about the body, skin, muscles and nutrition I knew I needed to take better care of myself, not weight related, more so my partying ways. I made the decision to stop taking drugs as I felt bloated, sluggish, tried and realised that the drug usage, although not as severe as some peoples I knew, it had really affected my metabolism and metabolic rate in terms of processing food along with my overeating in my younger years. I felt tired, run down and like the weight was coming back real quick.

I'm lucky I didn't really have an addictive personality, some may think I did because of how frequently I was taking drugs, but I was taking them because I wanted to and was enjoying my life at the time. But the day I no longer enjoyed it, and a bigger and better priority came along, that overruled it and took precedent.

The day I decided to stop drugs, I just did, cold turkey. I have this thing where I can do things for years like smoke, take drugs, drink or be addicted to certain routines, hobbies etc almost in an obsessive way…then one day, I just wake up and stop, like I have absolutely no care in the world for it anymore! Which, in this case, was a good thing when it came to the drugs…? (If only I had the same control with food and more importantly, sugar at that time too!)

As I entered 2010, giving up drugs and even smoking without a second thought for them, my boyfriend and I at the time decided to embark on a very Aussie ritual of back packing and travelling the world, hence the reason to give up the partying lifestyle we had once enjoyed and use our money for something more worthwhile.

We decided to move out of the place we were renting, which also happened to be one of the houses everyone came back to party at and stayed with our parents for a while to save money for the travelling fund. Naturally, as our lives were changing and going in a different direction to a friend's group, we didn't see some of our clubbing group as much, and also, we no longer suited some of their lifestyles of drug taking and partying as we didn't par-take in this anymore and were probably seen as the boring couple now who didn't want to come out anymore.

But to be fair, at the time, I didn't really care. We'd had our fair share of fun, and at that stage, I felt like I'd been partying for 20 years, and was now about to embark on the trip of a lifetime!

As life ticks on, you will always grow in different ways, so never fear losing people or things. You'll always have the memories to look back on, and as one chapter closes and another opens in your life, just think what could be in store for you on your next adventure.

Chapter 7
Around the World in 169 Days

And boy what an adventure it was about to be! But first, we needed money! So, for the next four months, we worked our butts off, saving for this trip which I couldn't quite believe was about to happen, it still seemed so surreal to me. I had always visualised going on this big worldwide trip, but I didn't know if I would ever get the chance to do it. But once we got the idea and possibilities of where we could go, we felt limitless.

We collected brochures and visited travel expos to help us plan our route, looking in to flights, hostels, visas and before we knew it, we had the first 2–3 months of our journey booked up and ready to set sail so to speak. The rest, we were going to 'wing it' as we went and see where the world would take us.

By the April of 2010, we had packed up all our furniture, belongings, clothes we didn't need and literally packing away our lives as we had known it, in to storage. We threw some belongings we may need in to 20-kg backpacks each, things we assumed we may need for the foreseeable future and literally took off to travel the world for seven months.

I still remember waking up at 3 A.M. on the 25th of April 2010 for my mum to take us to Kingsford Smith Airport in Sydney to catch the red eye out to Phuket Thailand to begin what would become one incredible journey across the globe spanning over 3 continents, 25 countries, more than 70 cities and over 30,000 kilometres. For this, I will be forever grateful I got that experience seeing the world, and experiencing so many cultures, countries and meeting some amazing people along the way.

I've got to say it was one hell of a trip and a massive eye opener to what is out there, that there is so much to see and experience in life. It's bizarre to me that some people choose to stay in the one place their entire lives and never get the opportunity to experience what's out there.

From starting out in Thailand getting the standard tiger selfie, caring for elephants in wildlife sanctuaries, we made our way through Asia in to Vietnam seeing it in all its beautiful glory and across to Hong Kong and China walking the Great Wall before crossing the border in to Mongolia, riding horses bareback, trying horse milk and staying in traditional Mongolian huts in the open countryside. We then jumped on the 'Vodka train' to cross the Trans-Siberian Railway all the way across Russia, taking five days to get to Moscow. Yep, that's right, living on train for five days straight sleeping in bunks and drinking Vodka with the rowdy Russia soldiers. (Damn what an experience!)

From exploring Russia, then in to Europe through Estonia, Finland and then down to Turkey to chase the summer sun across the Mediterranean over to Greece, then by boat to Albania crossing the border into Montenegro via taxi, to which the driver thought it would be hilarious to pull bags of sugar out of the boot of his car yelling 'Droga...Droga' at the crossing point, pretending it came out of our luggage! Well, he found it funny—the border control guards didn't...or us for that matter. I didn't fancy spending the night in an Albania jail cell, and lucky enough, they realised he was joking, and we managed to cross the border.

Then on to Croatia and Italy, including the Vatican, then on route to Spain to watch a bull fight in Barcelona and then join in the festivities at 'La Tomatina' in Valencia, then to France eating lots of cheese and croissants under Le Tour Eiffel, then via train over to Germany to enjoy Oktoberfest, and probably the most beer I've ever seen or drunk in my life! Before hiring a car road trippin' around Austria and the Czech Republic, then a train ride to Switzerland, Liechtenstein and Luxembourg before hitting up Amsterdam in the Netherlands seeing the crazy Red-Light District and famous cafes, as our last European stop before heading over the pond to the United Kingdom. Finally, after 169 days, we had arrived at our final destination: London!

As we travelled, explored each country, visiting multiple cities in each, we didn't drink an awful lot and tried to make our money last as long as possible, just enjoying doing the touristy things and a few things off the beaten path, enjoying the sights and cultures, foods and people.

We were walking around a hell of a lot and on our feet for most of the day. I was burring off calories without even thinking about it, enjoying our carefree life as Aussie backpackers.

We ate on a back packers' diet mainly, but did enjoy some nice meals as well, tucking in to local cuisines, cakes, pastries, fresh fruit and street food. During this trip, my weight fluctuated up and down but I still carried a lot of weight on my stomach, arms and thighs in particular being around 90 kg at this time. But I didn't care, I was living life like a dream, not knowing really where we were off to next, no responsibilities, no bills to pay, no one to tell us what to do, just living so free and enjoying life. I was in my element, loving each day not knowing what we would discover next. I really am a girl that can live with minimal possessions and materialistic items, as long as I'm rich in life, culture, moments and memories; to me that's real wealth!

As we reached our final destination, landing in to London on 11th October 2010, it would be here that my life was set to change drastically (both good and bad), but I just didn't know it yet...

Feeding a leopard in Thailand

Riding a horse in Mongolia

Smoking Shisha in Turkey

Seeing the ruins in Athens

A night in Santorini

Riding mopeds around the Greek Islands

Sightseeing in Pisa, Italy

Seeing Venice by Gondola

Enjoying the festivities in Oktoberfest in Germany

Enjoying waffles in Belgium

Arriving in England, October 2010

Chapter 8
Living the New British Lifestyle

As we settled in to life in the UK, back came the responsibilities of life…AKA, time to find a job and make money again, I sighed to myself. Adulating.

We originally stayed at a place in Peckham, South-East London, job hunting day by day, travelling around the city registering with countless recruitment agencies searching for any kind of work. Our initial plan was to work for 6–12 months, save, then backpack our way back to Sydney via a different route, seeing even more countries.

We eventually moved to Berkshire at my nan's house in Windsor, the same house my mum had once grown up in with her six brothers and sisters before she had left the UK for Australia when she was 21.

I had a call from a recruitment agency in Reading at the time and after an initial interview to work for them as a recruiter, I had a second interview in one of their main London offices. The interviewer at the time told me to get a cheap suit, especially a jacket for the interview, as this would make me look more corporate and professional and the directors liked that kind of look for their consultants. (I groaned on the inside, I hated—hated—with a massive passion—suit jackets!) My arms were bigger than most people's thighs, jackets were just not made for bigger girls. Knowing I was still on a back packers' budget as well and the fact I would try my hardest to wear the jacket as little as possible, I ventured to the local Primark in Slough to buy the cheapest suit jacket I could find. After sifting through the sizes on the rack, I picked up a pair of size 14 (wishful thinking) and then 16 trousers and matching jackets to try on. It was the hope that the 14 may fit, but in reality, I knew I would probably need the bigger size, and yes, I was right. So, I purchased the size 16 £5 trousers and £10 jacket and off I went for my final interview on the train towards London.

I got offered the job just a couple of hours after the interview and was so excited that I accepted—this meant income! I was now a working woman again! But what I will always significantly remember about that purchase, is not that it got me my first job in the UK, is that one month on, I was bursting out of the trousers and I think the suit jacket was never worn again, as I could barely raise my arms over my head in it, and it was just too damn uncomfortable. So, it sat on the back of my work chair for probably a year or so collecting dust. Within four weeks of being in the UK, I was packing on the pounds again, literally right before my eyes, it's like I blinked and I had gained 5, then 10, then 15 kg (33 lb) all of a sudden in just one month. What?!

As the weeks went on and Christmas came, I looked as round as a pudding! Now putting on weight and ballooning up and down was nothing new to me, but this was almost too drastic for even what I was used to my entire life.

That drastic change of walking around for 3–5 hours per day on average whilst travelling, probably burning anything from 300 to 1,000 calories without even thinking about it and eating reasonably well, to now virtually no exercise and back to the routine of eating set meals, and almost just eating out of boredom and bad habit again, slipping in to the old routines.

After the trip of a life time, settling in to an unknown country we were getting on our feet again and not knowing many people or having our groups of friends here and previous lifestyle that we knew like the back of our hands. My boyfriend and I found ourselves at home a lot on the weekends and especially after work, as it was the colder wintery months here in the UK and mostly miserable and raining outside. So, I would often find myself curled up on the couch after a long 10-hour day at work watching TV, or browsing social media, instead of out exploring or acting like the tourists we were—or rather had been for seven months. We almost didn't quite know what to do with ourselves here in the UK, it really was a mixture of a massive lifestyle change and culture shock all rolled in to one settling back in to jobs but in a completely new environment to the one we had in Sydney.

We had really got right to work, and living like responsible adults again, taking on very busy full-time jobs in order to save money again with the hope of a second world trip back to Sydney in a year or so.

And that's how 2011 ticked on really. I would have to say this was probably a work-life balance I wasn't exactly used to. The UK working world was a lot more corporate and serious than I was used to in Sydney, working the odd admin, sales or customer service job here and there to make money in my early 20s. Or maybe it's that I was just getting older and life was becoming more serious compared to what I had in Australia, where I was more focused on living, having fun and just working to pay that old partying lifestyle I once lived!

Although, eventually, I realised the long hours were worth it as I saw my first few pay checks coming in and monthly bonuses working in recruitment were too good to be true. I threw myself in to my new job as I eventually discovered I was actually really good at it, with the gift of the gab, sales skills and my love for helping people, I found I was working 50–60-hour weeks and actually loving it once I got stuck in to it and knew my way around it all.

Not really doing much else during the weeks, I turned in to a right workaholic, but I didn't care, the commission was great, better than great, it was more money than I had ever made in my life and at only 25, I was loving it.

After visiting 25 countries on our trip, I had the travel-bug as they say, and decided England was a perfect spot to live and work from and use it as a base to see so much more of this beautiful amazing world we live in.

So, without further ado, we started planning our next trip to some of the European cities we had missed out on along the way and decided on Norway, Sweden and Denmark for a mini 11-day trip over two back to back long weekends we were getting here for the royal wedding. It was a great little break away after our big whirlwind trip, and made me want to work even harder to keep ticking countries off the bucket list. I decided, at this point, I was going to visit 80 countries before I turned 80, as the world really has some amazing places! (To the present day, I'm still going for that goal—currently 44 and counting!)

It was following this trip back in the UK, I was sorting out all the photos, as a vivid amateur photographer I took thousands where ever I went, always with a camera at the ready, but upon viewing those photos in the April of 2011, around 6–7 months since arriving in the UK, it was then I really realised I had piled on the weight! This wasn't exactly a shock as my clothes were getting tighter and tighter, and yep, those size 16 trousers I had brought back at Primark in Slough were stuffed at the back of my wardrobe somewhere. I was well in to a size 18 now, and to be honest, busting out of them actually not even able to do up the top button anymore, and about to buy some new size 20 clothes, "…hey, summer was coming soon, why not get some new clothes?"

After all, I had moved to the UK with only the clothes in my 20 kg back pack, I really did need a new wardrobe full! And that's exactly what I did, along with spending my hard-earned money on holidays and trailing adventures, I grew an addiction for online shopping.

This new fad of being able to buy whatever you wanted online in the UK was a lot bigger than it was in Oz when I had left and I was fascinated at how easy it was to select so many items (available in my size for once, as it didn't stop at size 18's anymore—all the big clothing shops almost made it too easy: "Your clothes don't fit? Hey, don't worry! Presto, go up one more size…" Some of the plus size retailers were like never ending, size 28, 32, 36).

So, as I grew bigger and out of one size, I would just buy the next size up. I would order varied sizes of 18s and 20s to try them on, keep what I wanted and simply return what I didn't want. This was so much easier to me than going in to store and rumbling on the racks for clothes that I was pretty sure would not fit as most stores only stock up to size 16 or 18 on occasion. So, this meant I could still have pretty much any clothes I wanted and didn't have to go anywhere! Online shopping to me was simply amazing, I almost become addicted to it! OK, correction, I did become addicted to it. I think I was spending about £500 a month on new clothes and our wardrobe was getting full as I wasn't really doing anything with the old clothes, they were just piling up on the racks, like my own clothing store. It didn't seem to occur to me at the time that I should think about doing something about my size instead?

As we approached our first UK summer, we had already planned our next holiday abroad and this time, it was Nice, in the South of France! Yippee *SUN,* I thought to myself! After months of cold British days indoors, I couldn't wait to lie there topping up my tan and soaking up that vitamin D whilst sipping on cocktails under the sun's rays. *Heaven!* I thought. This was the life.

This also meant I could treat myself to a few new bikinis. I remember being amazed that stores like New Look, BHS and Simply Be had size 20 bikinis online, just what I needed for my summer holiday! What, you didn't think I would wear a one piece just cause of my size, did you? No-Sir-Ee! This Aussie girl loved a good tan, and that involves minimal tan lines.

I wasn't shy to be in a bikini and this was played out on the first day in Nice. As we grabbed our stuff after breakfast and headed up to the rooftop pool that overlooked the long stretch of beautiful beach front which made up part of the French Rivera, we set ourselves up on two of the sun-loungers, wearing my new coral bandeau bikini. I remember grabbing the sun cream and coating myself in it ready for my day of sun worshipping.

As I rubbed it in to my oversized stomach, rolls, stretch marks and all, I remember seeing a mother and daughter to the left of me staring, jaws open and all. They were gobsmacked whispering to each other and looking back and forth at me and down at my stomach…

Now, without jumping to conclusions, I had seen this look and action before, it was nothing new. I could tell exactly what she was saying to her slender young daughter. I'm sure, without a doubt, they were horrified I was in a bikini at my size. Even as the mother pointed directly at me, I wasn't put off I kept rubbing in that lotion! Mum always told me not to get burnt!

As I was returning their gaze, looking directly at the mother and then daughter, I raised one hand from my lotion application and waved a big old bingo winged arm at them, and with my typical Carli smile, I loudly said, "Heyyy!" And with that they quickly looked away with embarrassment, pretended they were talking about something in the distance and returned to their own business with flushed cheeks and looking sheepish…

I know my happy friendly reaction may not be the same as everyone else's…I've always been quite open, direct and let's just say unique to how I've dealt with being big and my life choices with my body. It was nothing new to me, no denial or shock about it. I was big, yep, overweight and obese and I knew it! So, in true Carli fashion, you guessed it, I didn't care in the slightest. I was happy, enjoying life! Hell yeah, I was in the South of bloody France without a worry in the world and god damn this girl wanted a well-earned cocktail and a tan! Nothing was going to put me.

I had never been ashamed of who I was or what I looked like. That was that mother and daughter's problem not mine and their stereotype issues, I wasn't there hurting anyone. I would likely never see them again in my life after that holiday so why would that moment bother me or ruin my holiday? I chose to be exactly how I was, wear bikinis and bear all, what was the big deal? This is me, I thought, I'm happy with who I am, living my life to the fullest, loving every inch of my body, and with that thought, I lay down and didn't give them another thought. I don't even remember if I ever saw them again on my holiday. I have a great ability to block things out, almost unintentionally, but hey, 'outta sight, outta mind', right!

Chapter 9
Let the Good Times Roll

As the months went on after that holiday, it's all a bit of a blur to me now. Work, eat, sleep, repeat was my life, like a routine, living to work so I could travel or shop. They were literally my two pass times and hobbies now. I kept on working away, and doing as little activity as possible, I was still putting on weight and going up a dress size every 4–5 months.

I significantly have these images of how big I was getting in my head from 2011 to 2012 maybe because I took so many photos, that's almost how I have catalogued everything in my life and have such a good vivid memory. Like a photographic memory literally. For anyone that knew me growing up, especially in high school, they can vouch for my love of capturing moments. I was always the girl carrying around a camera, like those old disposable ones we had, before camera phones and digitals and all that. I always had one in my school bag to capture any moment with my friends. I was also never shy being in a photo, and never one to delete ANY, no matter how big I looked in them.

I know a lot of people who hate themselves in photos either A) won't get in the photo in the first place, B) delete all the ones of them or C) crop themselves out of them…that was never my style, I love memories, and deleting or cropping yourself out doesn't make the problem go away! You know you're still there in real life, people can see you anyways.

I remember a friend of mine from Sydney coming over to the UK to visit in 2011, and I remember thinking how big I looked next to her in the photos. I was like twice the size compared to when we were in our high school days (and I thought I was big then, geeez, I wish I was that size now!).

It was my 26th birthday the following month, and we spent the night out in Wimbledon, partying away with some friends including one of my best friends in the UK, Cheryl, and again, I remember seeing all those pictures and thinking how big I was next to her, my face looking really chubby, my stomach rolls visible in my clothes, but yet, I always looked so happy, cheerful and carefree. I wasn't necessarily comparing myself to the others in the picture, it was more realising how big I was getting. Like when I saw it in the photo, it was real, as I actually didn't own a full-length mirror in my home, just the square mirror on the bathroom wall, that was the only other time I really saw myself!

I think, by now, I was just so accustomed to getting bigger as the months passed by, that was normal to me, like it never crossed my mind, 'Hey, why don't you do something about it?'

As Christmas drew closer and NYE went by, it was the same thing looking at pictures in that way and as we went in to 2012, I was slowly creeping in to a size

22, but that was cool with me. You know, I could just buy more clothes and the 20s got pushed in to the back of the wardrobe along with the size 18's and 16's…(I think I literally thought this wardrobe was magically, like stepping in to Narnia…endless space as the clothes got further and further pushed inside).

This year saw a week-long getaway to Morocco. So, again, new bikinis were brought, from M&S this time, and although they were tight and a rather snug fit, I just loved them and brought them anyways. I can still see this image of me in the pool, enjoying myself, but growing wider in the camera frame, my arms looking like they were ready to burst.

During our trip to Marrakech, we walked the markets, sampled the local foods and even went on a camel ride, and now, this I remember vividly, thinking the poor camel baring all my weight, and when seeing these photos, I could really see my size growing, barely recognising myself, yet that didn't stop me enjoying the all-inclusive resort each day, and most importantly, the food on offer, sampling it all, like food was going out of fashion.

Then later that year, I went to Amsterdam and Ibiza with a girlfriend from work as back to back weekend Euro-trips, and again, more new clothes were brought, and yet again, I saw the holiday snaps of how big I was next to my slim framed friend. Also, being aware of how much I ate compared to her during our meals across the weekend as I saw my plate next to hers…

I think these were the first pics that I didn't just realise how big I was getting, but how unhealthy I looked now as well. My skin looked bad, I looked lethargic, frumpy, and generally just not good at all. It almost reminded me of how I looked back in my drug filled party days, almost…

I had always carried being big well, confidently, dressed well for my size, but for once in my life, this was the point I realised that I didn't think my size now looked well anymore. It' was almost like my size couldn't be disguised anymore by my big smile and fun go-getter lifestyle or by buying the latest trends in fashion no matter what size I was going up to next…

And it was like suddenly, after all these days working to afford holidays, buying clothes, and then looking at photos to bring it to reality on repeat each year, started to make me realise where my life was heading, and yes, despite having fun and doing what I wanted, I was just year on year getting bigger and bigger, and I think a tiny-incy bit of my subconscious started to kick in at this point and I was becoming aware of what I had become accustomed to with my body, weight and health over the last 20 or so years of my life…

Chapter 10
Sydney... Oh That Place Called 'Home'

As the months of a new routine and life in the UK had gone by, I couldn't believe it had been over two years since we left Australia on our big travelling adventure.

Everyone kept asking when we were coming home but the word home was so confusing to me now. From a country I had grown up in and never knew anything different for 24 years of my life, I now felt a very big attachment to Surrey and the UK where I now lived. That is a feeling I never thought I'd ever have for another country as I had always imaged Sydney being where I would live my entire life, grow up, have children, and grow old there as naturally that was my home. But it didn't feel like that anymore.

So, it was, that we decided to go back for a visit in November of 2012, but we also decided to permanently relocate all our goods that we had packed in to storage almost two and a half years earlier, and bring it back to the UK with us. We were about to tell our families, that actually, we weren't coming 'home' and that we had made the decision to stay in the UK for the unforeseen future.

As I always used to stay and still do 'why break what's not broken'. We were enjoying our jobs, making careers for ourselves and loving using the UK as a base to travel from, and so we made the decision that we would now settle here, for good!

As the months approached, getting closer and closer to going back to Sydney, I suddenly felt very conscious of my size, not self-conscious, just conscious of how big I was, from the girl who had never ever had self-esteem issues about her weight! I knew I had packed on the pounds, and there was no way of hiding it, even though all my friends and family knew I was big, overweight, etc...but this really was bigger than I had ever been in my entire life.

I thought to myself, *'Wow, wouldn't it have been amazing to have gone home slim, skinny, small and everyone be amazed at how much I'd lost...* but no, that would never happen, look at me, I was always going to be big. I WAS the big one, always had been, always would be...who was I kidding?

****

As we approached the 14th of November 2012 and the long anxious flight home after not seeing anyone for years, I remember landing in Sydney, feeling nervous when I really should be so excited, and the familiar smell of the air was nostalgic, yet revoked such odd memories and feelings all at the same time...

I know my mum had seen photos of me, but I think she was shocked at how big I had got during my time away. On second thought, correction, I knew how shocked she was, you could see it on her face. Mum never was very good at hiding what she thought through facial expressions.

As everyone greeted us 'welcome home', they were saying, I couldn't help but feel that this didn't feel like home anymore, and I didn't know why. I was almost disappointed at that thought, as my entire life, I always thought the little town of Balgowlah Heights and Manly Beach would forever be home…but for some odd reason, I responded in my head to myself, 'No, Surrey is now home, Carli'.

We made our rounds catching up with friends and family over the 14-day trip and I knew people must have been thinking, 'wow, she's got really big', even I was thinking that. It was then I realised the last two and half years had gone by in a whirlwind travelling adventure whilst working away my life that even I suddenly realised where had the days gone, working, growing in size, what was I doing with my life?

Yes, it all seemed great and fantastic travelling the world and don't get me wrong, it was. I don't regret any of it. But what was I actually doing? Like what was I doing with my life? Where did I want to be? Was I happy? Was the UK about to permanently become home?

All these questions started flooding my mind, racing thoughts. It's like coming back to Sydney after so long had made me think about my life and all I had done since taking off. I started evaluating everything we had done and accomplished, and also starting to think anxiously about what I wanted to do going forward. It was all so real now that we were in Sydney packing our lives and belongings in to a shipping container and the reality kicked in that I was leaving my comfort zone and safety net of what had always been my home town and really making a new life for myself in the UK.

Slightly nervous as anyone would be at 26 years old leaving everything they ever knew for a new life, had just hit home. Even though, yes, I had been in the UK for over two years, it's almost like it was fun and games, we were backpackers, working, saving and travelling and one day maybe returning to Sydney, because simply we could. We had Sydney to fall back on if the UK didn't work out. But no, now we had made a commitment, we were permanent UK residents, and even though still anxious about this, some spark inside me thought this was a good thing, despite how anxious I was, and change is always exciting as you never know what's in-store when you step outside those comfort zones…so, with my positive attitude, I wore so well overruling the negative doubting thoughts, I knew deep down inside everything would work out. What's meant to be is meant to be really!

As the Sydney trip came to an end after the 14-day trip, I remember sitting on the plane returning to Heathrow and thinking that I actually couldn't wait to get back to our little home in Surrey, get back to my routine, even to work and my life as Sydney was behind us now. Surrey was where I now felt at ease and comfortable, my routine and the life I had now created for myself was there waiting with open arms!

At the rooftop pool in Nice, France

Riding a camel in Morocco

On holiday with my friends in Ibiza

Nervously jetting off to Sydney, Australia, 2012

Sydney, Australia, 2012

Sydney, Australia, 2012

Chapter 11
Let the Cycle Continue

The year 2013 arrived at full speed and it was a new year and of course new adventures to plan…New York, LA, Vegas, Mexico, Dubai, I thought to myself. The possibilities for the next 12 months were endless. It was like we looked at a map and just pointed out where ever we wanted to go! Then we went!

As we settled in to what was essentially really our new life now, no longer backpackers or one-day-maybe heading back to Sydney people, we were now adopted Brits!

I continued to work my life away, literally, and earning the money to match, I would eat my days away in the office sometimes working 10–12 hours each day. But I was comforted by knowing I had an exciting trip coming up, holidaying every three months seemed to now be the norm, and it's almost like that kept me going at the end of each quarter in my hectic recruitment job. To be fair, it was worth it, seeing all these countries and getting to vacation as often as I did was amazing, I was incredibly grateful and counted myself lucky. I loved knowing that my hard work did pay off and I can happily say to this day, I still cherish every country I visited and the memories I made along the way. In essence, I was doing what I wanted to do still.

Like they say, if you want something in life you have work for it, and I really was! At that moment in time, I was still riding the travel-bug wave, enjoying exploring the world and all it had to offer, in between adulting and working my full-time job.

****

But since my boyfriend and I returned from Sydney just a couple of months earlier, with all our belongings on-route in a shipping container heading for the docks of the UK, ready to really settle down here as a couple, suddenly, our relationship at the time was not going so great.

I guess like people say, your mid-20s is when you find yourself and grow as a person. After all the travelling we had done together, and had now settled in this country away from our comfort zone in Sydney of family and friends and the life we once knew, we had come out the other side in to a new reality and were almost two different people, growing in different directions, who had hit a rocky patch in our relationship.

I found out early 2013 about a lot of lying, cheating and general crap that you get when relationships go sour…you know, the usual turmoil that can end any relationship. I could go in to more detail here, but this book isn't about relationships or a bad romance novel, so I won't bore you with soppy relationships tales. Instead, I'll keep this short and sweet. We'd come to a point where it was very clear that obviously, we were not happy being together anymore. Done deal…right? Geez, I wish it was that easy LOL!

But I think in some ways, I didn't really know what to do about it. I know the obvious advice any girl would give her friend is 'leave his sorry ass', which yes, is sometimes easier said than done. I felt awful ending it after moving all our stuff to this country together, but then why should I be unhappy and miserable because I felt bad ending it, when he had done what he had done? I felt guilty if I did end things as my partner at the time would have had to go back to Australia as he was here on a de facto dependant visa on me. How did I know if I was making the right decision? Could I manage here on my own? Would I regret it and want to be with him again? Could I forgive him and carry on, see if it works? All these questions running through my mind, I didn't really know what to do, and he begged me to try make it work…and so, we carried on as we were. Unhappy. Together.

I don't know if I was comfort eating even more because of that, or just from my normal habits and boredom with the rest of my life in-between holidays. Probably more the latter. Boredom. Although the travelling was amazing, the three months in-between trips is almost a complete blur of my life and what we actually did with our time.

We never did anything during the week after work, and pretty much nothing on the weekends except the food shop and watched TV from the comfort of the couch. It's like we would watch 20–30 hours of TV between Friday night and Sunday evening. Just two box-set junkies morphing in to the furniture, snacking and eating away the weekend.

Life was becoming miserable, I suddenly felt I'd lost part of myself, the fun, happy go lucky girl I had always been, the ray of sunshine as I often got referred to. It was only really on holiday, carefree and away from life, that I genuinely felt good, like the me I knew so well.

I think I had masked this person through my workaholic days in-between holidays thinking it was all worth the money, bonus and consequently the trips. I realised, despite living a great life, travelling the world, having a good job, this wasn't right, between wasting away the days and weeks doing nothing or sitting at my desk working, eating, getting bigger and bigger—either way, I thought something had to be done soon!

I'd wake up each day and consume probably 800 calories just for breakfast consisting of massive bowls of cereal, or toast, maybe a muffin or pastry as well and glass of OJ or Starbucks coffee! Then snack away the morning at work on biscuits, chocolate, fruit, yogurts…and it usually wasn't even 10 A.M. yet. By this point, I'd added probably another 500 calories to the day!

This would be followed by a massive lunch of salad and chicken, or 1–2 sandwiches, or sometimes, pre-made pasta meals, usually with dessert consisting of another thousand calories in total here. Then afternoons spent picking at snacks with the team in the office of chips, nuts, chocolate, cakes…whatever was lying around and caught my eye fuelling another 600 calories mid-afternoon, then home to eat dinner, usually a double portion of steak or lamb and veg, sometimes pizza, or homemade curries, and then yes, even more dessert, sometimes two. If I couldn't choose which one I wanted, I'd just have both. By the end of the day, I would easily be over 4,000 calories without even realising it at the time…

Chapter 12
Binge Eating

Binge eating was at a whole new level, even to me, and I was feeling more and more tired each day, literally dozing at my desk by 11 A.M. I found myself going on more and more cigarette breaks, trying to wake myself up and get away from my computer, but I'd end up feeling ever more lethargic and out of breath as I walked up the one flight of stairs back to my desk each time puffing swaying with exhaustion. That being the only physical activity I did every single day.

Getting home by 6:30 P.M. each night, I would fall asleep on the couch within minutes, head nodding off. *Why am I so exhausted?* I thought to myself…maybe I had diabetes, or an underactive thyroid, I pondered, thinking of any medical reasoning it could be…

I used to do the whole Dr Google thing frantically searching for things that could be wrong with me, answers to my weight or health problem. Like 'Carli, it couldn't be the simple fact that you were morbidly obese by any chance, could it?' No, surely not, I think to myself, sarcastically, as I type this now! Coming up with every other possible health reason it could be, bar the obvious! I had never had any major health issues or problems and hey, I ate healthy foods too right, just lots of it. So, I assumed there must be some underlying issue causing my weight and obesity issues, right? It's like reasons could slap us right across the face, and we still want to blame something else, instead of taking responsibility for our actions and life decisions.

So, off I went to the doctors instead, and got tested for diabetes, just to make sure I was OK, and sure enough, I didn't have diabetes. From memory, I don't think the doctor really gave me any recommendation or health advice. He just tested me like on auto-pilot and a quick phone call for the results a week later, saying I was clear, and that was it.

I think during 2013, my subconscious was starting to conjure up some courage in the back of my mind to take on my carefree attitude one day soon, piping up every now and again, knowing I really needed to do something, but it's like I had no care to at all. That whole losing weight thingamajig looked like a whole lot of effort I didn't have.

I liked my food way too much and quite frankly, I was damn right lazy. My body was lethargic, and I didn't even know where I would start. Besides, as if I could lose weight, I simply couldn't even imagine it. It's like I thought magically, one day, I'd just grow out of it or stop growing finally, yet doing nothing about it and continuing to eat the way I did in excess of 4,000 calories a day.

I was literally like a bottomless pit, constantly chewing on something, like a chain smoker addicted to cigarettes. I was never without food, like an addiction in itself, but I didn't quite know that then. It's like I had this fear of missing out, I had to eat everything in one-day, inhaling calories like there was no tomorrow, not even tasting it. I can still hear this saying my mum used to say to me when I was younger shovelling mouthfuls of food in to my face, "Carli, slow down, it doesn't even touch the sides, chew your food slowly!" Now, I'm thinking, 'God-damn, Carli, stop chewing all together' LOL.

Meals were gone in seconds, I always remember, while eating out with friends, how quickly I ate compared to them. I used to try eat so slowly when out at a work-do, or birthday dinner for fear of finishing my meal before everyone else, as it was so embarrassing how I demolished food.

From how quickly I would eat, in those initial five minutes, my brain never registered how full I was, and that initial taste made me want more, and I would gorge on second helpings, then from all the saltiness, I would want something sweet and start devouring the nearest treat in sight, whole packets of Jaffa cakes, a box of muffins, block of chocolate, whatever was around the house or office. All this before my body had time to send signals to my brain saying, 'stop, stop, you're full'. I was beyond full, but it was too late, I'd already eaten way too much, but that was nothing new to me.

Even times when driving, stopping for petrol, I used to dread the thought of going in to pay, as I know car eating was such a weakness of mine, like eating with in the comfort of my car no one can see me and it doesn't count right. The service attendant would see me coming a while away '2 for 1 on chocolate bars, Ma'am?' as I was already reaching for my selection, plus usually a bag of chips and maybe an ice cream too. Not that I even needed or sometimes wanted some of this stuff, it was more a really bad old habit I'd picked up and never shaken.

To this day, I still do dread going for petrol sometimes, just the thought of the old me, although these days it's very rare for me to buy anything unless I actually want it and need it. I think last time I stopped, I actually brought blueberries, realising that small thing is a massive achievement to me, a non-scale victory so to speak!

I used to binge eat to the point of feeling so full and sick, but usually, 20 minutes after, I was looking for my next victim in the cupboards or fridge. It's crazy now to think how I consumed so much food, but obviously, I know where it was going, straight to my stomach, thighs and arms, that's for sure, but how was I consciously doing that?

One scenario I hated being in, was free food, especially at work cake-bake days, birthdays, and weddings. It's like I hated the thought of wasted food, and had to try it all. I couldn't help myself, I knew deep deep down inside I should walk away and avoid avoid avoid! But no, it was like I was a hyena going in for my prey, anything, even foods I didn't really like. It was free, right, you don't want to waste it!

Like ground hog day, I'd wake up the next day and do it all over again, and what do you know, more food. There was never that practice of 'save some for later' or 'have that tomorrow'. I always had to consume it then and there.

This is probably one of my worst old bad habits and to be honest, has taken the longest to overcome. Even to this day, as I write this book, I may get the one day in a blue moon where I still feel like this, and want to just eat everything. And sometimes, if it's a time I've been really good, I do allow myself treats and indulgences, but when it's not time for that, those pesky binge urges usually come when out and about, without my normal food at home, or set meals and confronted with temptation that I was not expected or prepared for. Although I have learnt to control it over time, training myself and my willpower.

Now, this may not work for everyone, and it won't happen overnight, but I do have to remember there is still food tomorrow, you don't need everything in one day.

Step back, take a breath, close your eyes, and remember why you are doing this, the long-term goal, not short-term cravings.

Try to picture how you will feel after the binge, you know it's not worth it, visualise what you really want for the long-term. I then often have a good 500 mL or so of water, which often can just make the craving subside for a moment, as 9 times out of 10, when hungry, we are actually thirsty or lacking a certain mineral or vitamin our body is actually needing.

After the water, you have a chance to change the scenario. I try to say no altogether and wait for a proper meal or opt for a healthier snack of something else to take the craving away and know deep down that is better for my overall goal.

Now, for anyone who has never been in a binge eating scenario, they may not understand the lack of willpower here, and the urges that literally possess a binge eater, but for anyone who has, I suspect that is the majority of people reading this book, that you know what I mean, and yes, it sounds easier said than done, but you have to practice what works for you and not always give in to cravings and binges. We are stronger than we know and have the willpower. Visualise how proud you will be sticking to your food plan, and that tomorrow is a new day.

Food addiction is actually one of the worst addictions you can have, alongside sugar addiction. And I say this because we're told to control our food and not eat all the bad things that society puts in front of us, but since kid's food is everywhere we turn, shopping malls full of KFC, McDonalds, Pizza joints, cake etc…

Supermarkets aisled with chocolate and chips, movie theatres with sweets and lollies for days, the list goes on! Everywhere we turn, since our brains were developing as children, is food, food, food…so trying to overcome food addiction when you are surrounded by it sometimes takes more willpower than non-food addicts realise.

It's like a cocaine or heroin addict, I know these are more severe, but say for instance we say, get healthy, come off drugs, but we are going to surround every shop and place you go to with cocaine and heroin, the supermarket, petrol station, movie theatres, shopping mall, sports events and you still have to partake in using it every day, but quit at the same time. Do you think they could resist or give up?

Again, I know very different addiction in itself, I'm just using it as a comparison. When food is everywhere, and we see adverts and cheeky marketing campaigns shoving burgers, chocolate, soft drink ads everywhere you turn—trains, magazines, gyms, social media—the thought of food is around us every day as we have to eat, we have to consume food to survive, but faced with the bad types full of processed additives, sugars, fats and chemicals and our minds and dopamine hormone liking them gaining a dependency, it's hard to get it out of your system.

To this day, I still do online grocery shopping so I only buy what I need to fuel my body, not what I want, or the old me wants rather when faced with too many temptations all at once walking around the supermarket.

But again, like any addict, you will find a way that works for you to overcome situations, cravings and those really bad urges, and it may just be a trigger that gives you a big old wake up call to stop and get healthy one day!

Chapter 13
Self-Awareness: When Life Gives You Lemons

Holidays came and went throughout 2013, even though we were unhappy in our relationship, we tried to make it work and still went away together as that seemed to make it all worth it.

Yet again, the photos would be there to show me just how big I was getting after all this binge eating and this year. I was up to a size 24 by May of that year. I remember buying these brand-new dresses for my up and coming trip to LA and Vegas, they were great, but I thought when would it stop? I had discovered new online retailers that made sizes 18–34...a 34! Geez! Oh, but I would never be that big, would I? As if I wasn't big enough, my arms had always been big, but now, they were huge, probably bigger than most people's thighs.

In the back of my mind, I knew my health was at its worst physically on the inside as well as out. I was still enjoying myself and life as a whole, as never one to be too gloomy or negative, I actually ended up having a great time in Vegas, still wearing bikinis by the pool, sipping on cocktails, and appreciating the life I had. I always thought, *Hey, things could be worse girl,* I always thought to myself. *You live a good life, roof over your head, you have a good job, two arms, two legs! Just enjoy it!* And so, I did, this was me and how I would always be!

****

Fast forward the next few months and as August approached, I was about to go on the most anticipated holiday yet, 10 days, all inclusive, in Mexico! I was so excited, just the break I needed! (I swear, I do work in between LOL)

It didn't disappoint either, it really was an amazing destination, and you don't need to even guess if I brought new bikinis and clothes for this summer holiday, the answer was always yes! I was now on the verge of a size 26, and about to find out just how big I really was, weighing myself for the very first time in years in the hotel room in Mexico after a very indulgent breakfast and a little self-realisation as well...

****

And here we have it back to the very first opening paragraph of this book, the all-important catalyst moment in my life that changed everything...not instantly, but I think I will always have the visual in my head of standing on the scales in that hotel room in Mexico, I remember the beige colour tiles the wood trim of the vanity, the scale beneath my weight, attempting to see my toes hidden by my protruding pregnant like stomach (I'm surprised no one ever asked me when I was due?)

I don't know why, for years, I was so comfortable with being big? Was it my no-nonsense approach to life, being confident and happy with who I was since young, society making it so easy to be big these days, life and work taking over, bad habits and comfort zones I couldn't break (more like didn't want to break), or always being told, 'you're big, it's hereditary'... I think the answer is all of the above!

I was content and a little too comfortable, I didn't necessarily want to change, or was just too lazy to. I also enjoyed food a little too much, as you can tell from my recollections throughout this book so far, and I'd always done what I wanted, had a boyfriend and great friends, living an amazing life, I felt blessed and thankful, so hated to whinge or seem ungrateful for my own choices...I did genuinely love who I was and my body, despite, over the previous year, coming to a little self-realisation that I needed to do something about my size, I still never hated on myself or got down about my weight. I just appreciated who I was, going about my life day to day.

So, that day in Mexico was almost like my first slap-in-the-face of how big I really was stepping on the scales and seeing 127 kg come up.

Between the trip to Mexico and my big wakeup call that day in February where I actually finally decided to do something, there was one more occasion, that was gearing my subconscious to wake-the-hell-up and realised I needed to do something. Like all these things were screaming at me, 'Carli, when will you actually take control of your size, you don't have to be big anymore!'

For my 28th birthday that same year after Mexico, I went to Dubai, a few months later, and being the daredevil I am, the number one thing on my bucket list had always been to skydive. And not just any old skydive, jumping out over a field or something, I wanted to do Skydive Dubai, one of the most famous locations in the world to dive, jumping out over the palm and ocean for miles! What an amazing experience I thought, and what better way to celebrate my upcoming birthday.

So, in true Carli style, once I got the idea in my head, I just had to go for it, and I quickly started googling SkyDive Dubai to find out all the details and book it in advance of the birthday vacation. But as I started reading the rules and guidelines, disappointment started settling in, *What?* I thought, *I can't do it! I was too big!?*

News to me, majority of skydives have a weight limit, and I was well over, 37 kg over the limit in fact, but not only this, Dubai had a BMI limit as well, and my BMI number wasn't even on the BMI range. I was well off the scale, past morbidly obese...

This was one thing that really got to me, as I have always stated, my size has never set me back in life, never stopped me from doing anything. I always did what I wanted, when I wanted. But no, not this time, girl...you're too big! And for once in my life, I couldn't do what I wanted. (Insert every sad face emoji possible here!)

I still went to Dubai, and funny enough had to drive past the skydive venue on more than a few occasions and could even see people jumping from the sky from our hotel. It was like a little reminder every day from up above, saying, 'this could be you, but you don't care about your body and weight, Carli, remember'. To this day, I can still remember my disappointment inside at not being able to tick this off the bucket list, I was gutted. That was slap-in-the-face number 2.

Then that last day in February 2014 and that feeling of being paralysed was like my 3-times-a-charm-slap-in-the-face, saying, "OK, this is it! Girl, we see you holidaying here and there, then coming back to your life, bad habits and routines in between, well no, not this time! Carli, remember those scales from Mexico! Remember not being able to skydive, yeah them!" Well, now my health was also telling me, "Get the hell up and do something before you have a heart attack!"

I realised I couldn't carry on, working 60-hour weeks, eating, going up a dress size, then going on a holiday to make it all seem worth it and fair on my body and health! There is no comparison or compensation there. I can be whoever I damn well want to be, living life, but I knew I just had to do it at my healthiest! And so, came my big decision to lose half my body weight all on my own…

Chapter 14
The Start of It All

As mentioned earlier, the first few months of my journey in 2014, ticked on and I was amazed at the results I was seeing. Was this really me? I had always pictured my life as the big overweight girl and never did I think I could be slim or even lose 1 kg let alone 20, 30, 50!

A few times, I think I pinched myself, was this really happening? I know it all sounds silly but it's all sort of surreal to me, some people will never get what I mean, I can't explain it, but when being obese your entire life, accepting it for what it was and thinking it wasn't possible to lose weight, to finally getting those results, I had only ever dreamed about or seen in weight loss stories in magazines, it really was like a dream come true.

Now, I know that all sounds odd, but it comes down to the mentality I had grown up with and lived with my entire life. I was my own road block, my limitation, telling myself it couldn't be done, or rather I couldn't do it, and then hearing that from family, society, diet companies, it almost set it in stone in my mind. I guess in some ways, accepting it, and owning it made me the confident girl I was. There was nothing wrong with being overweight and fat in my eyes (except for the health issues I was eventually made aware of). I was happy, go lucky and carefree. But on the flip side, I know there are a lot of people who are overweight and miserable, unhappy, and get very down on themselves. So, in some ways, I was lucky that I had such a good outlook on my body and size. If there is any positive I cherish from the first 28 years of my life, it is that it made me live life to fullest, not caring what people thought of me, I lived and let live, literally every single day!

But sure enough, the day I changed my mentality and realised I too could do anything I wanted, was the day I realised I could also have anybody I desired. My number one priority was now me, and I decided to take the 1–2 years leading up to my 30th birthday to be selfish so to speak, to spend time on myself and get healthy, fit and of course shed the pounds.

Along with this new outlook for me and my healthier life, a few months into my journey during 2014, I eventually ditched the boyfriend too, in case you're wondering LOL! I couldn't stay in a relationship for the sake of it constantly trying to make it work, and being so unhappy, there was a lot more to it, and it just kept getting worse. I had to be my own priority, miserable didn't suit me well, and I had a better life to live without him in it.

I knew this new me, meant sacrifice, but when has anything in life so great ever been achieved without a little sacrifice, hey?! I knew this meant cutting back on drinking, slowly cutting out the cigarettes, less late nights out with work and the usual Fridays down the local pub and maybe even less holidays, but all of this, I was surprisingly OK with. These things weren't important to me anymore. I'd found a new passion and love for life, and most importantly found some extra love for me!

See, when you have a dream that you know you can come true your priorities shift and as if overnight my entire lifestyle changed, but only because my mentality already had. What the mind believes, the body will always follow.

I knew that if I took just a couple of years to get fit and healthy that I could have a completely different life as well, a life of better quality, for more years to come than my life expectancy could of been had I kept getting bigger and bigger.

Who knows if I hadn't of woken up that way in February 2014 with pins and needles, if I would have actually ever done something about my weight, as just that week I had brought my first size 26 dress from New Look, to which I never wore, and sold instantly on eBay knowing I now never would.

If I hadn't made that decision to shed half my body weight, I could well be a size 30 by now or worse off health wise. I'm sure by my mid-30s I would have had a heart attack or something equally as bad. One of the things in my bigger days I used to actually fear the most about my size was that one day I may have had to buy two air plane seats on my next holiday as my butt was pretty much too big for just the one and flights were becoming so uncomfortable. Thankfully, I never came to that situation either.

As I got down to that initial mark of about 113 kg, it spurred me to keep on going. Each day was a chance for me to better myself, my health, and my overall well-being. I kept saying to myself, *think of your circulation, your lungs, your heart, your cardiovascular system, all your internal organs, Carli,* as they were all literally thanking me right now on the inside. It wasn't just about the transformation on the outside and how I looked physically, but really, it was about the inside and how much better I was feeling!

I was truly in charge of my happiness, no longer was I doing everything to please others and just routinely ticking on each day at the mercy of my work, my partner, friends, responsibilities and the 9–5 life. I knew I would get the best out of life now and people would get the best from out of me if I was healthier and the best version of me that I could possibly be. This thought was making me even happier than I had realised I could possibly be.

Even though I was never really that unhappy, to me this was ultimate satisfaction, self-accomplishment really knowing I could achieve what I set my mind to. It's almost like the willpower and results were the addictive part and the true secret to keeping me motivated, but really, no secret at all, we all have the ability to gain self-motivation and belief which turns the gears to turn that willpower we all have inside us. You just need to find the power and passion to use it, see we are all born with willpower, but you might train it to be strong, just like any muscle in the body.

I was still working away in the recruitment job, but I'd come to realise I wasn't as passionate about it as I once was. I was my new passion! I didn't need to live and breathe it anymore like I'd done for the previous years, as I knew my health was now far more important to me. So, I made my work-life balance a priority, trying to get out on time to make sure I could fit in my exercise each evening, getting up from my desk more at work, going for walks at lunch time, even just to the local shops or around the block, trying to be more active than I had previously been back in the day.

I still treated myself to little holidays now and again, and within two months of the new healthier me, I was jetting off to Sharm El Sheikh in Egypt all by myself. Being in a different place with an all-inclusive buffet, I was conscious to not eat everything insight like the old me would have done, and to not fall off plan, as so many people do when going away on holiday, letting themselves go.

I made sure I picked a resort with a full gym, so each morning I got up early and worked out for about an hour then ate a healthy protein rich breakfast. During the days, I relaxed, read, swam and snorkelled to keep myself occupied and tried not to drink so many cocktails like I used to. I realised it wasn't even forced, I actually liked getting up early and embracing this new healthier type of holiday. The rush of endorphins waking me up and having that feel good feeling throughout the day, less tired and less lethargic really was paying off and made it easier to stick to my new goals.

Along with my first holiday in a slightly heather state, this was the first holiday I didn't go up a dress size! Instead, I had come down three dress sizes to a size 20, and to me that was just amazing as never in my life had I ever gone down a size and of course, the new bikini's I brought for this trip were smaller too, simply because I had to, none of the old ones fit!

As I returned to life in the UK after my break, I was more aware than ever to keep at it this time and not fall back in to any bad habits or old routines.

As the weight kept coming off post-holiday, it was more and more addictive to me to see how far I could go with this, and the results I was seeing each week in the mirror were keeping me motivated to find out.

Chapter 15
Getting to 100 kg

In June that year it was to be my mum's 60th birthday, so I thought what a great way to celebrate than to meet her half way between Sydney and London in the bright lights of Vegas to celebrate!

As we grew ever so close, I was so excited to see her, but more so as I had been telling her over the phone about my new healthy lifestyle and weight loss goal! I could hear in her voice how proud she was that I had been going to the gym and eating well (but also some slight hesitation and scepticism in her voice, making sure I was taking care of myself, not doing any of these silly fads, and probably wondering would I stick to it this time, as she knew I had always struggled with my weight and tried so many weird gimmicks over the years with no real plan to stick to them at all).

I was determined to prove I could do this! So, I had set myself the goal of getting to 100 kg, or even better just under 100 by the time I got to the USA, and so far, I was well on track!

I was feeling so proud and happy with myself. It's like anything I set for myself now, I just knew I could get there, no self-doubt would ever creep in this time round! *100 kg*, I thought to myself. *Geez! I can't remember being that weight for such a long time, yet that would be 27 kg down in the first 3–4 months,* I thought, visualising it to myself! (Again, pinching myself, yes, I was really doing this).

I set off one day to do a bit of pre-holiday shopping (yes, I still did this) but this time was different! This time was the first time ever I could go in to store to buy clothes. Gone were the days of online shopping from the corner of my coach at home! I had to go in to the store as I genuinely didn't know what size I was in some of the shops anymore, and for the first time ever, I could finally buy River Island clothes! This might sound non-exciting to some people but to me, this was a non-scale victory, as it was the one shop I used to only be able to browse past online, or window shop, knowing they didn't do my size (as they didn't have a plus size range back then), yet I loved their clothes!

This is how long I hadn't shopped in an actual store for: I remember getting to central London supper excited at about 10:30 A.M. to beat the crowds one Sunday morning, to realising the shops didn't open till 12 P.M. on Oxford Street on a Sunday?! *What, 12:00 P.M.?* I thought to myself. Yes! Laugh at me all you want, I had lived in the UK almost four years at this point and didn't even know what time the shops opened on a Sunday. So, instead, I grabbed myself a coffee and waited with anticipation eagerly for the shops to open as if this was like the Boxing Day Christmas sales to some people! But to me, it was even better than that.

Finally, at midday, I walked through New Look, River Island, H&M, Topshop and tried on various items, so excited that I was a size 18 now in most, but even a 16 in some stores! "What? A size 16," I squealed to myself! I was amazed, this was like a new found high to me, goodbye online shopping addiction and *helllo* my new love for trying on new clothes in front of the changing room mirrors. I think I was even just trying on clothes for the sake of it now, admiring my new figure in various items of clothes, simply because I damn well could!

I then went in to Nike and decided to buy my first pair of brand new sneakers in years, hold back, make that at least a decade! These were like a reward for all the endless miles I had cycled so far in my crappy old moccasins and treating my feet to some new kicks to embark on many more miles to come! (To this day, I still have this pair of Nike 5.0 free runs, and I don't think I'll ever be able to throw them away no matter how worn-out they get) Bright pink and purple in shade, I was so excited that I then needed new gym wear to match. So, yes, I brought a few bits and pieces to go with it. I loved being able to look at items of gym kit and image training in them working out, fascinated by all the items and colours I had been missing out on for so many years as well as seeing how far gym clothing had come since I was in high school. (This is where I developed my obsession with matching gym kit, leggings, cute tops etc...and if you've followed me on IG for a while then you get my drift here...)

When I got home that day, I decided I really want to increase what I was doing physically and up my exercise soon, as what I was doing was almost becoming so effortless and easy to me, I had to up the ante. I started to look in to gyms to join when I got back from Vegas, to make sure I really stuck to it post-holiday again. But in the meantime, to keep my routine fresh and mix it up a little, I purchased a few more bits to add to my 'home gym' buying some heavier dumbbells and kettle bells. At this point, I could really feel my passion for this growing, I was loving being activity, increasing the time and intensity of my workouts, eating even better, cooking healthy meals and generally just feeling good and positive about myself.

Life was good. Plain and simple, I literally was loving this new lifestyle, and most importantly, the new and ever-improving me!

Chapter 16
Vegas, Here We Come, Baby!

I still remember the moment my mum walked through the arrival hall doors at LAX airport. She was so cute wheeling her case along in excitement looking for me, eyes darting everywhere before she eventually spotted me amongst all the other receivers of family members and friends waiting for their arrivees. Tears in her eyes, we hugged and I could see she was looking at me oddly up and down. After all the months of me telling her over the phone about my new healthier lifestyle and commitment to my body goals, she eventually told me that she couldn't see a massive difference, but yes, that my face and arms looked slightly smaller…

I had been telling her about my weight loss journey every time we spoke on the phone, but I guess for her, all she could picture was the big me when I had visited Australia back almost two years earlier in 2012, and since then I had packed on the pounds in the years since then, and now come back down. I was probably only slightly smaller than when she had seen me in Sydney. I guess not really the reaction I had been expecting, as I was so excited by my new good habits, but for my mum, she had known me my entire life as overweight, so for her, maybe she couldn't see my vision just quite yet.

Following that initial reunion and embrace, we had such a great time in Vegas! I did let my hair down a bit, after all the work I had done the months prior, we enjoyed eating in nice restaurants, having a few cocktails and of course desserts. I did, however, have a bit of a conscious deep within and an actual craving to still be good. After all, I wasn't doing all this hard work to be able to eat the same or more, I wanted to lose weight and be healthy, changing my lifestyle. I didn't want bad habits to come flooding back, or just eat for the sake of it like I think people do sometimes, especially on holidays. I had to ask myself in every moment, what did I want and what did I feel like? Don't eat the cake just 'cause that's what you used to do.

Now, don't get me wrong. I think you should treat yourself, if you want it, not because that's what people think they should do on holiday, there is a difference there. I was due to be away for 13 days, and it bugs me when people say, "Oh, live a little, eat what you want, you'll burn it off." I hear what they are getting at here, but I'm not training and exercising to reward myself with food; I'm not a puppy! I'm doing this to better my body and I made the decision to sacrifice things, but I realised it wasn't sacrifice at all, if you didn't actually need or want the foods in the first place. So, my message here is don't force yourself, if you actually don't want something, but it's more of an old habit or peer pressure, then simply don't have it!

I enjoyed my new healthy lifestyle, genuinely, and often, I found myself questioning whether I was just eating and drinking certain foods out of habit, in holiday mode, as well in the company of my mum, as it was like tradition from my heavier days we would always enjoy a good meal out, or cake and coffee together. So, I decided, yes, I can enjoy myself within reason but still keep at my routine as it was a lifestyle now, it was literally part of me and my routine, and I actually did love the new life I was leading in to.

That's something I think people need to embrace and live by when doing a journey like this. You really can have both: a holiday and enjoy yourself, still doing your new good habits and routine!

So, with that in mind, I swear I must have been the only person in the whole of Vegas walking through Caesar's Palace casino floor, decked out in my new Nike trainers and matching gym kit, sober as fuck heading for the gym at 6 A.M. one morning when I couldn't sleep feeling jet-lagged, while most Vegas visitors were just coming out of the clubs and bars heading for their rooms at this time. I even had party goers and slot machine zombies staring at me like I was in the wrong place. "Is this girl for real?" LOL! Yeah, I can enjoy a good gamble and night out and still get up and gym-it the next morning!

Again, this wasn't forced, I actually wanted to go, and since my time zones were all outta-whack, and I couldn't sleep, I thought why the hell not, my body was aching for it. It was enjoying the extra movement and activity I'd been doing recently and it was missing it.

This is when I really realised the saying, 'listen to your body!' I knew it would make me feel good and probably even enjoy my holiday more, starting my day right and the only way I now knew how to do. I can still see the image in my mind of me walking past all the drunken party-goers, gamblers at the slot machines and tables, cashier ladies sitting in their windows falling asleep, as little old me, fresh faced and feeling good power walking through the lobby with determination all the way to the gym. *Who does this in Vegas?* I thought to myself. Me, that's who!

A few mornings, my mum even joined me in the gym for her own routine workout, and I could see the expression had changed from that of the airport a few days earlier, to now one of belief and faith, in what I had been telling her was all true. She could see I was enjoying this and embracing my new gym ways!

Although I can tell you I still did love my food, being a foodie will never leave me, but this time, I had much better control over it and of course, a better understanding and relationship with food!

Especially whilst in Vegas and knowing very well of the all famous all-you-can-eat buffets! So, those big morning gym sessions were also a way to compromise enjoying the holiday whilst still enjoying my new healthy lifestyle. To be able to try some of those buffets guilt free, sampling various foods and dishes, including having a few indulgent foods out of the norm of my new food regiment, but also actually eating a lot of healthy things as well, eating without worry or having to calculate everything, as my new relationship with food was that of a more healthier one! A far cry from the buffet in Mexico on that holiday, many moons ago!

As the days went on, enjoying ourselves out and about in Vegas, playing the slot machines, shopping, seeing a few shows, it was one day we had a small win on the machines, and Mum treated me to a ring from one of the jewellery shops, but

67

what was more significant about it than just it being the only sentimental piece of jewellery I own still to this day, is the fact I could walk in to the shop and before even trying it on, I knew it was now going to fit my more slender fingers, than it would have months earlier, my fingers then more resembling fat sausages. Some people may not get this, but when you can now confidentially walk in to shops without your subconscious fatty saying, 'nope, girl, don't even bother, it won't fit you, they don't make sizes for you', I smiled to myself and wore it out of the store, staring at my hand and shinning new gold ring in awe, anyone would have thought I'd just got engaged LOL!

After a week in Vegas, we then made our way back to LA for a few days sightseeing there too, as this was my mum's first ever time to America, so we did the whole touristy thing including shopping on Rodeo drive. Again, I could enjoy this knowing I could go in to stores and actually try items on, including even getting a few pieces of sportswear and lingerie from Victoria Secret, and not having to think twice about picking up sizes.

We had a fabulous time together, and it was one of the first holidays where I felt genuinely me, making decisions for myself, and embracing my new good habits! As we came to the end of that week, it was soon time to depart and go our separate ways back across to other sides of the world.

I remember saying goodbye to my mum at the airport and a very emotional one at that, both with tears welling up in our eyes and endless hugs. I think we both knew that we had no idea when we would see each other again, what I would look like then or what the next chapter would hold for me…

So much had changed in just a few years and I knew she worried about me and missed having me back in Oz. But my mum always said I was the wild crazy one, wise and older than my years. She knew I had always been 'Miss Independent' and I would be OK back in the UK following my heart and most importantly, my dreams and goals.

I still have that image of my mum in my head, waving good bye to me down the corridor as I walked off to my gate to head to my now home of London.

Chapter 17
Gym Life

I got back to the UK and right back in to my healthy life wanting to really stick to my routine and not do what so many people say they do when getting back from a big vacation and falling back in to bad habits and days off from their new lifestyle. No, not me, I was actually craving to get back to my little home, routine and, of course, good habits, right back in full swing. Hey, this girl had goals to hit and no time to waste!

Knowing I had indulged in the US, I stepped up my workouts and exercise time. And boy, did it pay off! I was dropping the weight again, knowing the little change in eating even better, cutting out more bad items, replacing them with better options was all working in my favour.

I wanted to increase my routines and vary my workouts, adding more weight training sessions and different types of cardio, so I could be exercising every day, without fail, kicking those fat burning hormones back in to gear post-holiday. I remembered the idea of joining the gym. So, with my new-found attitude to follow through on anything that would help me go forward with my goal. I went online, brought a day pass for the local PureGym and decided to try it out. (I had not stepped foot in an actual gym in almost 10 years since I was about 19 or 20 back in Sydney!)

I know, for a lot of people, entering the gym was scary, daunting, intimidating…but for me, oddly enough, it actually felt so natural, like coming back to an old stomping ground I once vaguely knew from my younger years of actually being introduced to doing sports and the rowing training I once did, eventually enjoying it too. (I do sometimes kick myself for stopping after rowing in high school!)

As I entered my pin code and walked on to the gym floor, I was confident. I didn't really notice who else was there, I wasn't actually bothered; people never intimidate me like some women have often said to me about 'fit' people in the gym. Instead, my eyes were darting about, observing all the equipment, cogs turning in my brain at all the things I could do here, observing the machines, recognising ones from my teenage years when I had frequented fitness first a few times here and there with my rowing squad. I was going in to overdrive with excitement about exercising, yes, I said that, excited about exercising!

So, I made a beeline for the change rooms, dumped my gym bag in one of the lockers, eager to get started, and off I went to the row of treadmills to start warming up as I wanted to try out different equipment to vary my routine from what I had been doing at home on the old cycle bike.

I had just popped in my headphones ready to get going with the tunes flowing in to my ears, when a very over keen personal trainer jumped on the machine next to me trying to get my attention, arms waving about, all ready with his sales pitch, probably noticing I was new, and probably also seeing I was overweight. I think he thought I could, hopefully, be his next new client...but, oh boy, was he about to be told otherwise...

Sales-man mistake 101—don't assume you know why someone is there, or buying a certain product or service...a good salesman will always ask their needs first then adjust his sales pitch with a solution to suit their needs...

But no, not this one, he went straight on in to some pros and cons about the gym, what he could offer me (not knowing anything about me), assuming I was just getting started and that he had all the answers to help me out...not wanting to be rude, I didn't interrupt his spiel, instead I just kept smiling, then when he was finally done, waiting for me to say 'sign me up', I just said, "Thanks but no thanks, I'm not looking for a PT, I've lost four stone already by myself, I'm good, thanks!" With a further polite smile, I put my headphones back on, as his jaw just closed and turned to seek out another person in the gym, and off I went walking and jogging the next 30 minutes away kicking off my first gym workout as the new me.

I then decided to try out a few of the leg machines, hip abductors, leg press and the dumbbells and kettle bell section. I must have been in there for a good 60–90 minutes and was satisfied this gym life was definitely for me. So, I signed up online and made sure this wasn't going to be a fad, trying to get there at least three times a week plus working out at home every other day. Making sure it fitted my routine, around work, so there were no excuses not to go, and for once in my life, there wasn't. I was actually making up excuses to go to the gym and saying no to going out with friends drinking.

Soon, a very keen regular in the gym, it was like my sanctuary and respite time. A new good habit I did without even thinking about it, I drove there on autopilot and never once thought about diverting or putting it off. I eased myself in, teaching myself about the machines, using Google and YouTube to research new exercises and routines I could try for various body parts and muscles. I was researching every night how the body worked, seeing what exercises I could do for each muscle, what reps and sets would give me the best response rate, how to shape and define my body, as well as looking further in to cardio and fat burning zones, stretch routines and even exercises on how to tone loose skin.

I set my self out a weekly routine, one day doing jogging and leg exercises, the next, it could be the back muscles and cycling, then arms and shoulders, or maybe, it was chest and abs. I would mix it up, keeping my workouts exciting and varied, as not to get bored or over-do one particular thing, as I have a tendency to do when I really enjoy something. I wasn't strict on time either, if some days I could only manage 30–40 minutes then great, I did that. Other days, like on the weekends when I had more time to play with, I may have done 60–90 minutes. It was all about how I felt that day, my energy levels and listening to what I wanted to do. But I tell you what, there is no such thing as a bad workout, and even on days I felt lazy, within 20 minutes in the gym, I didn't want to leave. You had to literally drag me out of there sometimes!

For any machine I wasn't sure of, I'd find out about it, instead of avoiding it, and over time, slowly but surely, I knew every machine there and what muscle group it was for, the benefits what weight increments were best for me, and simply educating myself on everything I need to know, as I was still determined to do this all on my own, educating myself and expanding on my bodies knowledge.

Now, I'm not saying PT's are a no go at all, lots of my friends are actually PTs and I want to actually do the course soon enough, more for my own knowledge. It was just a personal decision and more a commitment really, to not have one as part of my journey. It was more satisfying to me knowing I could do this. I've also never been good with people telling me what to do, yelling routines at me or motivational speeches, each to their own, some people need that, some don't and like me, I found I didn't need someone else motivating me, I was my own motivation to succeed. So, why pay someone else to train me when I was simply enjoying training myself and getting the results I wanted. So, why would I pay someone else to do that?

I wanted to prove that if you didn't have the money or resources to get to a super high-tech gym or pay for a personal trainer, you didn't have to and could still lose the weight. I hear so many people say to me that they can't afford long detailed programs, don't understand them, can't afford gyms or fancy memberships, so that's their excuse not get fit or workout. I wanted to do this as minimal as possible, showing you can always make something work if you want it bad enough, and you don't always need all these added things just to get healthy.

I joined the gym after the initial four months of working out at home and realised this was more than just my life now, it was a full-blown passion and hobby. I craved being at the gym, working out, exercising for hours on end…just like some people choose to read, some like gardening, socialising, going to the movies and lunching with friends, shopping etc… for me, this was how I now enjoyed to pass the time. It was my new favourite activity to do in any spare time I had.

I did, occasionally, still go out with friends, maybe once a month if that, but not drinking as much as I used to and maybe only a cheeky cigarette here and there as I had started to cut down a lot. I wasn't quite at that perfect my body is a temple mantra yet, but I was slowly giving up all the bad things over time, I had been putting in my body for years, not going cold turkey as I already knew this all was already a drastic change for me and my body as it was, so knowing me and how I react, slowly-slowly, is always the way for me with any change.

I think that's important to note. You have to know how you react to change and differences in your life. Some people prefer cold turkey, the all or nothing approach, and others need to warm to the ideas, make your body get used to the adjustments over time, till you don't even realise you've made those changes and it's ridden from your life without even noticing it's gone.

That was a big thing for most of my journey and transformation, me, getting to know me! What worked well, what didn't work, how I reacted, how my emotions and feelings are evolved, when to push myself, when to rest…it was all a trial and error to start with, really listening to myself and what I knew I had to do and where my inner voice had to take control and over rule some decisions, it really was a learning curve I was willing to embrace and be patient with.

This was all such a getting to know me period of my life, like a new self-discovery almost 29 years in, and I was really starting to love getting to know myself, my full potential and the person I was becoming.

As 2014 rolled on by, I kept up my healthy fit lifestyle losing on average a kilo (2.2 lb) per week to start with, as I ever so steadily increased my activity and exercise time and intensity week on week. (This ration did slow down as I got lighter, to more half a kilo per week.)

More and more people began to comment and notice the weight I was losing, and I think realisation had set in over the first six months or so, that I was really on this 110% and not stopping.

People at work were congratulating me, saying well done and without sounding big headed, they were commenting on how well I looked. For those people who had not seen me in a while, they genuinely looked shocked when I bumped in to them. It's like they double took and didn't realise it was me.

I was always known amongst my friends and work colleagues at the recruitment company as the partier, the drinker, the smoker, the life of any occasion…but now, I was making up excuses not to attend nights out, Fridays at the pub, clubbing, or any drink fuelled event really as I simply didn't enjoy that anymore and honestly would have rather been in the gym till midnight over a club any day! Believe it or not, that is actually how I spent a couple of my Saturday evenings, happily lifting away the night in the weights room. I remember one Saturday so distinctly, there was only about three of us in the gym and as I finished up my session around 11:45 P.M., walking to my car I thought to myself how life had really changed in only a matter of months and what a difference one thought could make…or the better of course, and I smiled knowing it really was!

People had never ever known me as the fitness junkie, it was like a 360 on the Carli everyone had known. People were even starting to ask me for advice on how I was doing it, what foods they should eat, what exercise I did each day, how I was keeping it up, and what I planned to do next…to be honest, I had no clue at that point, I was just taking each day as it came, going about my business, working on me, for me, and for once, just focusing on my life for a change.

I often thought that sounded selfish, then I remember no, if I wanted to enjoy life and years to come I really had to put myself first and stick at it, no distractions, no obstacles, carry on my path to my better self…like they say: "You simply can't fill up someone else's cup if yours is empty." Help yourself first in order to then help others more.

So, that is what I continued to do, working away on me, for me! Going to the gym, sleeping well, eating right, remaining positive and supporting myself every step of the way!

Chapter 18
Why on Earth Would I
Write a Book?

In October 2014, eight months in to my journey, I went on holiday to the Dominican Republic with a colleague at the time. We had purposely booked a resort with a great gym and leisure area as we were both in to keeping fit. So, again, each day on this holiday, I got up and went to the gym, even going back most afternoons, after a day at the beach.

It felt so good and so different, in a positive way, to the days of my old vacations, this was like I was away at some fitness or yoga retreat. I felt fresh, relaxed and rejuvenated, instead of frumpy and full of food and cocktails, hardly being able to move…I just literally loved this new me, still embracing life and doing me, just a much healthier version.

One of the days, I did a boat trip out to a reef in the middle of the ocean with a tour group, swimming and snorkelling with sting rays and sharks, not that I wouldn't have when I was bigger, I just felt more energetic and able, like there was no doubt in my mind I couldn't do these activities. My go-getter, try anything attitude was at a new all-time high now. I undertook activities without even thinking about them or questioning whether my size would handle them, or rather could they handle me.

After hopping out of the water, amazed at the experience, I'd just had of swimming in the middle of the ocean with these beautiful creatures, channelling my inner David Attenborough, it was then that I noticed the paddle boards! I had always wanted to try this, but would I be able to stand up, as this Aussie girl had never even tried surfing LOL! (I was shameful to admit!)

But hey, what the heck, what's the worst that can happen? I fall off, big deal I chuckled to myself. With my love for the water and knowing I was a strong swimmer I dived on in and free-styled out to the boards, and with one swift movement I hurled myself on to my belly and up on my knees… *Wow that seems too easy,* I thought, thinking the old me would have looked like a beach whale attempting that. Surely, there was a trick to this whole paddle-boarding malarkey, I'd seen all the celebs doing it off the coast of their Malibu homes in all the gossip magazines pictures. So, carefully and steadily I rose to my feet, trying to engage the core (I wasn't even quite sure I actually had yet…*note to self: introduce more ab workouts) and holding my balance, I stood tall and upright! Hmmm, no falling yet I thought, as I raised the paddle, I swung it side to side, the blade feathering through the choppy ocean water, left-right-left, balancing, holding my stomach tight, gripping the board with my toes, and sure enough, I was off, paddle boarding in the middle of the Caribbean Sea, so peaceful and serene.

I can still remember this feeling, I don't know why, but it was so euphoric, it just felt so great! An activity to some that may be like what's the big deal, but to me, it was just another notch of confidence, that hey, if you want to do something, change the mentality and just go for it. All alone in the middle of the sea, miles out from the shore, with just a few nets around us and old boats, I was standing tall on my board gliding through the waves.

Most things we decide we can't do in life before we have even tried them. It's all in the mind that is stopping you. Feeling pretty pleased with myself I paddled around for a while and then headed back in to the pontoon and nets to join the rest of the tour group. I remember one of the Dominican tour guides asking if I did this often back home in Australia, noticing my accent, and I told him it was my first time, and even he looked shocked. Tick.

The next day, I decided to go parasailing, even though yes, I had done this before in my teenage years on a family holiday to Bali, there was a sense of relief again with this that I wasn't as heavy as I used to be, the harness would fit. There would be no double take from the instructor questioning was my weight, or being over the limit, looking me up and down as I was so used to from any other similar activity I'd tried in my obese-days! So, off I went in the speed boat with the guides, loving it even before my feet had left the ground. I was always one for adrenalin sports, speeds boats or fast-action activities.

Just moments later, that was doubly confirmed as the wind whisked me in the air and I was sailing over Punta Cana high in the sky, feeling so comfortable and happy being able to experience these events, thankful for my healthier lifestyle and attitude to life as a whole. It was pure bliss in that moment and I was (still am) so grateful for opportunities like that, just to really experience life and take in all the surroundings.

As I was pulled back in to the speed boat about 10 minutes later, I just felt like no activity was a no for me anymore cause of my weight, I really could do anything I wanted! Really, I could!

It was around this holiday, and the following months as I returned home, as everyone saw me taking life by the horns and going for what I really wanted that a few people started saying to me that I should write a book about my journey… *Really?* I thought to myself. *Why? I'm just some overweight girl from a small town in Sydney losing some weight and getting healthy. Nothing special to see here peoples, anyone can do it, loads of people lose weight all the time…*

But more and more people kept saying it to me, even people I didn't know that well. Friends of friends who had told them about my weight loss success and go-getter attitude on life. I had a friend's mum's congratulating me, people at the gym, literally strangers saying to me, "I had to tell my sister about you, she's always wanted to lose weight," or "My mum has always struggled with her weight, she's got so big and doesn't know what to do anymore or where to start!"

Then there were comments that weren't just about my physical weight loss, it seemed more to the people than just my outlook on weight, it was my outlook on life and healthy living, being able to have it all.

I was working a full-time job around 50–55 hrs a week, no family or partner support living by myself, going to the gym 1–2 times a day, preparing and cooking all my meals, no programs to follow, no motivational support, figuring this all out on my own, whilst still enjoying life and on track to lose 63.5 kg (140 lb). From this, I think people were encouraged to know that you really can do this. You don't have to opt for weight loss surgery, gastric bands, weird fads you read about, crazy starving diets or pills; these are not the only options, so stop telling yourself they are.

I was just your average working girl, doing it my way, for me, and the best bit about it, it was working better than any fad you will ever see on TV or in the mags, and that's the bit people seemed to be amazed by…hey, you know that good old-fashioned way of eating well and exercising, yeah, well guess what it works!

I thought about people's suggestions to write my story, and then thought about it some more, and more again…and each week it slowly crept back in to my thoughts subconsciously, maybe I could write a book and share my story? We'll see, maybe one day I will…

Mexico, 2013

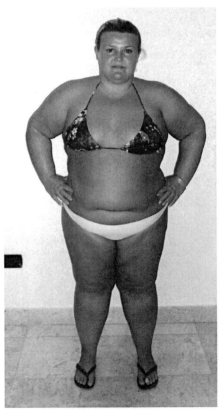
Mexico 2013, the first time I weighed myself in years

On the beach in Mexico

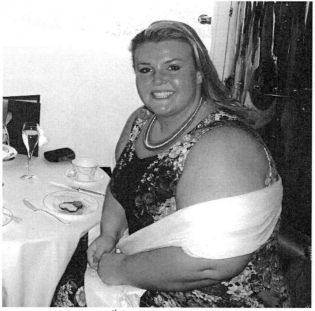

My 28th birthday, Dubai 2013

Paddle-boarding in the Dominican Republic, 2014

Dominican Republic

Meeting Mum in Vegas, 2014

Mum and I in Vegas, 2014

Chapter 19
New Year, New Me...and All That Jazz

As 2015 came in full swing, there was no stopping me now! If you thought I was already active enough, then think again, my passion was only just starting and about to grow bigger than I could have ever imaged.

My love for this lifestyle and being as healthy and fit as I could possibly be was increasing month on month. I started training twice a day, really kicking my ass in to gear! Sure enough, I got loads of people saying to me 'that's too much' or 'you're over training' and I'd think to myself, 'Too much for who, you or me?' It's funny people like to comment and put down when friends or even strangers are being incredibly active and yes, maybe exercising in abundance, but do they have the same through process and comments for themselves and their friends when out drinking, partying, or eating crap food? Yeah, I thought as much right! People are always quick to judge when we do too much of the good stuff, but I'm sure are the first to encourage and say to their pals, "Just have another drink you big softy, don't be lame!" or "Here, have a shot, down it, down it."

I knew how I felt, not other people, and the best bit was I was enjoying this. I kept saying it was a hobby to me, and along with that, exercising actually felt like rest and recovery to me, my 'me' time so to speak. It actually didn't exhaust me, if anything, it made me feel better. On the days I had a 'rest day', I actually felt worse off and still crave a leisurely walk or stretch session but to get my blood flowing. I was the only one I would listen to and take guidance from, not the opinion of others, especially people that didn't even know me, and passed judgement, more so from their own stereotypes or limitations of themselves. Sorry but you can keep boundaries and limits to yourself, you may not be able to go above and beyond, but I felt my body could. So, I did.

I wanted to get to that 50 kg weight loss mark real soon! Nothing would stop me, and with that in mind and my fitness brain taking over. I realised how much my work place was eating me alive, consuming more energy than I had for that job! The hours, the atmosphere, the people, it just wasn't for me anymore. It's like I started to resent the place, like we were robots, money making for them and our health and work-life balance didn't matter as much. So, since I had changed almost every other aspect of my life, I made the decision to leave that company and get a new job that more suited my lifestyle and out-of-work interests. Don't get me wrong, I still loved working in recruitment but wanted (more like needed) a different environment after the 4.5 years in the one place.

It was at that point I had a call from an old colleague working locally at an oil and gas company who needed a recruiter. His big sell to me was the gym on site. *Winner winner, chicken dinner!* I thought. Plus, shorter hours and flexitime, an employer embracing that employees actually had an outside of work life too, finally! So, I was sold, I resigned from my job in February 2015 and started at the new place in March!

Instantly, I felt better, a breath of fresh air. I was taking control of all aspect of my life for a better-stress free me! You have to be happy where you work and enjoy it, as we spend so much of our life there, and when you enjoy your job on the inside, it shows on the outside.

Getting up in the mornings was never a chore, I had a spring in my step from the moment I got out of bed each day. Getting to the work gym by 7 A.M., and still getting to my desk by 8:30 to start work was heaven, it was so good starting my morning that way and I felt good throughout the working day. Healthier and happier, enjoying my new job, I knew this was definitely a good decision and fitted with my hobbies, interests and sticking to the new life I was creating for myself and now lived.

I would then return to the gym onsite or my local PureGym after work for my second session of the day almost every second day, and still getting home in normal time to have a good meal for dinner and plenty of sleep. Life was good. I really could do it all.

I realised it was all about a good routine, and making this work for your lifestyle, it became like clockwork and new good habits, I didn't even think about where I had to be. I was permanently on auto-pilot...gym, work, gym, eat, sleep, smile and repeat!

Year 2015 was shaping up to be the first year in a long time that I was truly at one with myself, although it took me almost 30 years to get here, I was listening to myself, learning about myself, doing what I wanted, getting healthier, fitter and stronger, growing in to my best self and literally being unapologetically myself, just doing me and enjoying every single second of it!

Chapter 20
Never Take No for an Answer!
(If at First You Don't Succeed, Try and Try Again)

As the total lose so far of 50 kg was creeping closer, I really wanted to do something to reward myself or celebrate the momentous occasion, FIVE-0: 50 KG's! Like the size of a whole person in some cases! I'm not one of these people that loses weight then says, 'wow, well done, let's go out and celebrate with a big meal or piece of cake'. No, wrong idea, I'm not a dog, I don't reward myself with treats and food, especially when trying to change the body's fat percentage and weight. I want to mark the achievement with an event, something special to remember it by, in true essence of the word reward, and to be proud of what I have achieved so far!

The topic had come up of a short break to Dubai with a friend, and at this point, I remembered the Skydive I had wanted to do there sooooo badly for my birthday in 2013, and I instantly remembered the disappointment I had felt back then. *OMG,* I thought, *that's it, I'm going to do it now! I'm going to jump outta that plane!* The euphoria inside me was overwhelming, I could feel the excitement already, goosebumps all over me, and I hadn't even jumped yet LOL!

Most people get nervous about jumping out of a plane flying sky high in the air, but no, not me. I wasn't even slightly scared about it, I was ecstatic. Jumping out of a plane at 13,000 feet to me was the easy part! I was over the moon about that bit, but I was actually more anxious about the weight criteria and height/BMI check-in on the day of the jump, knowing that once upon a time, I was well over, and I was wondering would I make it this time?

The weight limit for females was 90 kg and under, which I was fine with as I was well under that by now, but in Dubai, as I'd found out last time, they also had the BMI limit, which I read on their website that they were very strict about and not to bother booking your jump if you were over their limits, as they would turn you away on the day with no refunds.

With me being so short at only 5'3, I was just above the BMI limit, despite being under the weight limit (bloody BMI chart, bane of my life!) But maybe that was the push I needed to keep going, past the 50 kg (110 lb) mark in order to get my BMI down too. So, without reaching the goal quite yet, but very much within sight of it, my friend and I booked the flights and hotel, along with the skydive, for four weeks' time, Monday, 4th of May. "YOU WILL be jumping outta that plane, baby girl!" I squealed to myself, anticipation running through my veins, just visualising the whole situation and how I would feel was making me so excited I couldn't concentrate!

As the days passed and the holiday was getting closer and closer, I was starting to panic just a bit, again not about the jump, but the weight check-in.

The departure day came and I headed for the airport to set off to the United Arab Emirates, I just couldn't wait to get out there and let the holiday begin.

Although once I arrived, I couldn't think about anything else. I was trying really hard to enjoy each day, we had three full days before the Skydive. I was stressing, my mind was consumed with the jump and my weight. I just kept thinking what if I'm over the BMI, what if I've put on weight since being here, enjoying all the food and drinks…

Even though I knew my weight and height at the time and thought I should be fine with the BMI, I was right on the verge of their limit still, and I did not want to be told for a second time that I could not jump. That would crush me, it really would. This meant more to me than just a skydive to the average person checking it off their bucket list. This meant so much more!

So, I tried to be so good, remain calm, whilst also trying to enjoy the holiday and make the most of the beautiful sites and activities Dubai has to offer. Going to the Burj Al Arab for an amazing spa day overlooking the palm, visiting the Atlantis Water Park, going to the top of the Burj Khalifa, heading out to a few of the famous nightclubs and generally trying to enjoy myself and not think about the skydive…

As D-day arrived and I woke up that Monday morning, I could not contain my excitement or my anxiety, both rolling in to one. I had butterflies in my stomach real bad, this nervous feeling was making me feel sick, and it was all for the check-in. It would be normal if I was nervous about the jump like most people! We got the taxi to Skydive Dubai around 7:30 A.M. to get there in plenty of time for the first jump of the day we had booked. *Nothing is going to ruin this,* I thought, praying for perfect weather and everything to go smoothly.

I had worn my white Nike high tops, just in case! (They gave me a few extra centimetres in height OK LOL!) When we arrived at the desk and had completed our weaver forms, sure enough the girl called us to be weighed and measured. I gulped and stood against the wall. *This is it,* I thought, anxious as hell right now, sweat beads on my forehead, palms clammy, my stomach doing knots…

I think I actually rose on my toes just a tad, and tilted my head up a centimetre or two, just to be sure, to which the girl didn't notice, thankfully! As the girl took my weight, she wrote it down on her clip board, then slowly checked the measuring tape at the top of my head, and wrote that down too, and then checking her weight vs BMI chart…she then stared at me with her blank face, and paused, which felt like an eternity, she then looked back down at her clip board…

Before marking a big fat 'TICK' on my check-in sheet and said, "Yes, you're all set to jump, thanks." *Whooooo yipppeee,* my inner voice squealed! (I've got tears in my eyes and goose bumps now just recalling this feeling. I get it every time, without fail, when I think about this day).

I remember right at that moment dropping down to my knees, anyone would have thought I was fainting, or been told no! I was literally so overwhelmed with happy triumphant emotions. Eighteen months on from my first try for this and I was about to do it. Finally!

All nervousness and anxiety had gone now, I could enjoy the whole experience. I remember having tears in my eyes and just feeling so happy and proud and my feet hadn't even left the ground yet. I must have been the calmest person in the venue after that, whilst all other eagerly awaiting jumper's nerves were just settling in for the ride ahead.

Now, all I wanted to was jump, to me the hard bit was over, the jump was the celebration, the victory to myself for all my hard work so far. Let's get this party started I wanted to scream at the top of my lunges!

I even asked if I could go jump first out of the plane (yes, weirdo I know.) The anticipation was exhilarating, all through the safety briefing and walk out to the plane I was grinning my big stupid grin from ear to ear. I remember my videographer and tandem jumper couldn't believe how happy I looked on the plane flight up to our drop zone, I was chuckling with excitement. The guy said to me, "Oh, we've got ourselves a giggler here!" He said he'd never seen someone so happy on the flight up, from the thousands of jumps he had done. He said most people looked scared or nervous, holding on tight, but he loved how I looked so happy and free to be there in that moment. And trust me that is exactly how I felt, and I'm glad he could see it.

As we soared higher in the sky with the plane door open the whole way up, I was just watching the beautiful view below as we flew higher and higher. The palm beneath us getting smaller and smaller, and all the cars and building looking like a SimCity game below us. As we arrived at 13,000 feet and hovered in the air, it came time to begin the jumps, and I was up first, and there was no hesitation there, I'd waited so long for this moment. I eagerly made my way to the starting position, hanging over the open door as we had been told to do, with my instructor giving me the final instructions ready for take-off. Then with a smile bigger than you can ever imagine, I thought to myself, *This is it, here we go, girl. 3...2...1!* I remember seeing the starter light go green, and that was our queue, as she tapped my forehead indicating we were good to go, we flung ourselves out in to the open bright blue Dubai sky!

The feeling was immense, an out of this world experience! Like nothing I can describe, or had ever experienced and felt before. To me, this wasn't just about ticking a skydive off the list, this was a real moment of accomplishment, so euphoric. Marking what I had achieved, from being not able to once do this previously because of my sheer mass to now feeling weight-less falling ever so slowly, yet fast at the same time, over the Dubai Palm.

I remember the adrenalin rushing through my body, not wanting it to end. I was trying to take it all in, the scenery, the experience, the emotions. I was so overwhelmed, but enjoying every second. Seeing the world from this very was amazing! The free fall was actually about 50 seconds, but only felt like 10, but then at the same time, it felt slow and calm because of the air pressure against us it was a real mixed feeling, then as we let the parachute up and floated down I got a chance to steer with my tandem jumper and really enjoy the whole experience, trying to savour it. But and soon enough, after about seven minutes or so we were making our way to the ground to land. Still smiling and even still giggling and squealing, like someone had just told me I'd won 1 billion dollars! I felt amazing, and all I wanted to do was do it over again and again! To this day when I watch the video of my jump, it takes me right back to that moment on that beautiful day in

Dubai, and I can re-live all that emotion, reminding me how good it feels to accomplish goals, and that feeling of satisfaction is what keeps me motivated, there is no other feeling like it!

I was buzzing, tingling all over, having an out-of-body experience, and I didn't want that feeling to stop. It was all so worth it, like I'm almost happy I got turned away in 2013. It made this time round so worth it, more satisfying and memorable, I really had earned it.

What a whirlwind morning. I needed a drink, that's for sure! And by 10:30 A.M., sure enough we were back at the hotel sipping on celebratory cocktails (hey, it was happy hour somewhere in the world right!) calming the adrenaline running through our blood!

We sat there for a good hour or so, re-living the experience, looking at all our photos and videos we got as part of the Skydive Dubai package, and I couldn't quite believe it had just happened. I don't think I'll ever forget how that whole day felt.

From that day on, I knew the sky was not the limit, literally, I could go beyond it, 13,000 feet beyond it, in fact, overcome anything, do anything I wanted, and that is exactly what I was going to go on and do…no limits, no boundaries!

Chapter 21
Wonderful World of Social Media

More and more people were encouraging me to write a book as I went on with my health journey, and I had also thought about documenting my journey, starting a new Instagram account showcasing my body transformation and starting to tell my story of how I did it. Almost like a blog, being able to answer lots of the questions I was getting from people in my everyday life.

I had a private Instagram and Facebook just for family friends, using it how most ordinary people use social media: sharing pictures, keeping in touch with people, status updates etc…nothing much to it. But I wasn't sure how people would receive my before and after pictures of my weight loss. I wanted to share them, as I was never embarrassed about it, but knowing me I'm very real and raw and don't sugar-coat anything. So, knowing very well if I was going to do this, it had to be so honest and real, open up about all topics, nothing was taboo for me. This way I knew I could really connect with people on a deeper level who were on similar journeys to myself and bring to light a real take on weight loss in the fitness industry today. I wanted to show how far I'd come and what I had been doing throughout my journey, focusing on major issues people deal with and potentially struggle with when losing weight or wanting to achieve any goal for that matter.

So, I decided to set up a fresh new Instagram page, public, for anyone to follow along that wanted to. But first, I needed a name, something catchy or memorable.

I had often been called Carli, Carli-J or CJ throughout school years, which was an adaption and take on my really first and middle name, but then I also wanted it to go with my new lifestyle and so, I finally decided on something that stuck in my mind, and just went with it:

@MissCarlijay_healthlyliving.

By June 2015, I'd set up the account and posted up my very first transformation picture on my new account without any idea of the response I would receive or what direction my life would soon take…

Yes, my friends and colleagues in really life could see me transforming, but I'd never got out my comparison pictures for anyone else to see, they were just something I was doing to keep myself motivated, but realised they could actually help someone else too, see it side-by-side in real life.

Over the coming days, I was posting 3–4 pics a day about myself, my journey, gym memes, inspiration pics, fitness ideas, motivational quotes and general health and fitness related tips on how I had gone about my journey so far.

As I woke up each morning to more and more notifications, I was shocked at how my Instagram was being received, the comments, likes and messages I was receiving was beyond overwhelming, I couldn't quite believe it. People were so supportive and encouraging and within a week I had about 500 followers, then my first 1,000 the next week and so on. It just kept growing before my very eyes.

Slowly, I started to disclose to my friends I had started this page, it hadn't occurred to me to tell everyone at first, almost like I wanted to see how strangers and the general public took it first before telling people close to me. It was like a trial, would it work? Would people like what I was posting?

I started sharing more and more about my journey, recipes, tips, lots of before-and-after pictures, and pretty much anything and everything that had been part of my transformation so far. I was about 16 months in to my weight loss at this stage, and as my page just kept growing month on month. I had about 10,000 followers within three months, I was shocked, this was more than I ever could have imagined. It was more so that people were interested in what I had done, and actually following along on my journey. I had always not thought too much in to what I was doing. Yes, I was proud and happy for myself, and had the support from people around me, but from complete strangers through social media, that was touching. In my eyes, I was just some obese girl that decided to get up and do something about her weight.

But more and more people were messaging me saying how they could really connect with 'the before 'me' pictures' and through my story, as if my posts were talking to them. Others were encouraged how I had gone about it, not trying all the fads this time and really showing my willpower, handwork and dedication. I was so pleased that these people were believing it could be done, and more so believing in themselves! Saying, "Hey, if she can do it, so can I!" and that's the exact reason I started my Instagram, with the hope of just helping one person realise their potential, be their best self, and enjoy the best life they could too, then that would make it all so worthwhile!

To this day, I'll always be incredibly thankful for social media and in particular Instagram, as even though there are people out there that loath the social media world and yes, there can be negative connotations with it, I do think, however, if used in the right way, it truly does have one hell of a way of connecting people around the world, making strangers not feel so distant, and that there are others out there going through similar situations to yourself, what even the life event may be, and that we are all closer than we know and sometimes not so alone with our issues, and that there are always answers and solutions.

Chapter 22
Training Here, There and Everywhere!

Instagram was now part of my life, and in a good way! Even though the newer generations will never know what it was like to not have social media, smart phones, cameras at the ready, and constantly watching people's lives at their fingertips on YouTube, Facebook, Snapchat, Instagram, but hey, as the world moves forward, so does technology, and sometimes, you just gotta embrace it and go with it, it's part of most of our lives now in some shape or form, and it's only going to increase in the future. Love it or loath it, I think I will always be a pro supporter of social media and the good ways it can be used as I couldn't believe all the people I was connecting with around the world, it was beyond amazing to me. Complete strangers sharing their similar stories with me, asking for advice and interacting with me through my picture and words.

I had also started connecting with so many fitness enthusiasts and likeminded people through the industry, not just in the UK, but across Europe, the US, Canada and Australia.

I was shocked at how friendly and supportive complete strangers could be, and believe it or not, some of these original strangers are now people I hold very close in my life and consider some of my closet friends today.

The fitness game was a whole new world to me and really interesting to try to understand and network around, and I was loving every minute of it!

It was around August that year of 2015, when one particular person reached out and asked if I wanted to train with him. At first, I was a little bit shocked. "Huh, are you talking to me, or was that message meant for someone else…" I think sometimes I still went back in to old big-Carli mind-set, like why would someone want to train with me? There are thousands of fitness people out there, the market is saturated with them. But then I had to check myself and be like no, this is you now, this is your lifestyle. This is YOU!

So, since I literally loved training anywhere and everywhere I was happy to train with anyone remotely interested in health and fitness, as a lot of my friends at the time weren't as in to it as I was, I naturally said yes. We decided to meet one Sunday at the gym formally known back then as the Reebok Club in Canary Wharf. As soon as I walked in, I knew I loved it, I was in was my element, it was spread out over three floors with a rock climbing wall, pool, basketball court and all the equipment you could possible image! Literally, like gym-heaven! I could already feel it was going to be a great session!

I met Charles in reception and it was like we already knew each other from being friends through social media. We couldn't stop chatting as if we had known each other for years, catching up over old times. We quickly dropped our stuff in the change rooms and headed to the gym floor to get started, as we had decided upon *legday*. We were working out as if we were old training partners, really throwing our all in the session, motivation and spurring each other on rep after rep.

Can you believe we ended up spending six hours that day in the gym, just breaking for lunch halfway through to give our legs a rest! I think to date that's the longest I've ever spent in the gym in one go LOL! Now, I know what some people will be saying right now, "What? That's too long, that's bad for you..." blah, blah, blah, yeah, I get it. But it wasn't just about the actual workout we were doing. It was more about getting to know each other, connecting with someone else who has a similar passion and embracing the whole fitness lifestyle. We talked about everything and anything to do with both our fitness journeys and paths in life and no matter how different we were, I realised we shared the same passion for wanting to be the best version we could be and chucking ourselves whole heartily in to this way of life. Some people may choose to go the local Westfield shopping mall and walk around all day for 5–6 hours shopping, well, yeah, we decide to gym-it instead! (And don't worry, we did good recovery after, stretched and had a protein fuelled meal—happy now?!)

From that day on, I grew this love of training with others and meeting other like-minded people, as for 18 months I had been training alone, not one single session with anyone else.

This then introduced me to a whole new world of people in the industry, and for each and every person I met and trained with, it was important to me to find out why they did what they did, their motivations, inspirations, reasons and journeys that got them to where they were that day. For everyone, it was something different, and that's what I loved, hearing so many different views on how fitness and health had helped and transformed so many people for the better, changing not just themselves, but their lives.

In September of that year, I then went all the way to Leicester to meet Taeo, another person I had initially connected with through Instagram, as we had a few mutual friends. Taeo was currently mid-prep for a men's physique and body-building show and invited me to come watch him compete at his qualifier show in two weeks' time. I'd seen a lot about this through social media and various fitness channels, and knowing the whole bikini fitness world may not be quite for me, I still found this avenue of the fitness world fascinating and what people went through, such strict regimes to get them to that stage was a great achievement. That levels of discipline and dedication was something I lacked for so long in my life, I knew I could take something away from this experience and even use parts to build my knowledge and commitment to myself, even if I wasn't a competitor.

Of course, I said yes, and I was right, I was amazed at what I learnt! The dedication that was felt from everyone I saw on stage that day was at a different level to anything I had ever seen before. As for Taeo's category, yes, of course, he came first that day, and I was glad I was there to support taking home that number one trophy!

This was just the first of many shows I then continued to attend across the UK, seeing so many others who competed, I realised it was more popular than I knew and I continue to meet more and more people, happily going along to support in various cities all over the country at many Body building and Physique shows.

During the last few months of 2015, my Instagram continued to grow, receiving so much love and support from people all over the globe and other bigger IG pages 're-gramming' my transformation pictures and sharing my story on their pages really helped and so I continue along my journey training twice a day, every day, sharing more and more tips and advice through my posts. It's like all my followers support was in-turn spurring me on to keep going every single day, and likewise, I was encouraging them to do the same.

20 months earlier, I never knew this is where my initial weight loss goals would take me. I'd woken up that day with the intention to just move my body and start getting healthy. I couldn't believe it, not just what I'd achieved with the physical aspect of my weight, but on the inside as well, how I felt, my lifestyle, activities, routines and day to day life.

I was just riding the wave and enjoying what life was throwing at me week on week. I knew my results were keeping me motivated and the excitement of this new life pushing me every step of the way.

With how Instagram and the general public was responding to my story, I decided it was time! In October of 2015, I started writing this biography, chapter by chapter, relaying everything that got me to the point of obesity and beyond, and everything that got me out of it.

Sky diving in Dubai, 2015

Skydiving in Dubai, 2015

Skydiving in Dubai, 2015

My 30th birthday, November 9th, 2015

My 30th birthday, November 9th, 2015, Andrea and Emily

My 30th birthday, November 9th, 2015, Emily, Laura, and Andrea

My 30th birthday, November 9th, 2015

My 30th birthday, November 9th, 2015, with Skye

The Sun photoshoot with the team in May 2016

The Sun photoshoot with the team in May 2016

Me enjoying the gym, 2016

Chapter 23
The Big 3-0

November 2015 had arrived! The all-important month, I was about to turn 30! "Eeek," I squealed! The big three-zero! Yep 30! The milestone age at which majority of people I know were either engaged, married, having their first, second, or some even their third child…

That quarter life crisis time period, that stereotypically so many of this generation go through, that you should be married with your house with a white picket fence and 2.5 children. But no, not me, I was quite content with my life so far. I was working hard on my dream body, health and life. No babies just yet thanks, I was more worried about my next gym session and weight loss goals, getting myself in check before pro-creating.

But as I was getting closer to the big day, everyone was saying, "Go on, you have to celebrate, it's your 30th!" But to be honest, I wasn't overly fussed, to me it's just another day, and at this time in my life, it seemed the only thing that really mattered was achieving my goals. But then again what, lame person didn't celebrate their 30th birthday? (I secretly really wanted to be that lame person LOL) Yet, I was convinced I should mark the occasion and celebrate, so I decided to go out with a few friends to the Hawksmoor in London for dinner and then on for a couple of cheeky cocktails at a friend's club in Knightsbridge.

Obviously, this special occasion meant a new outfit, and I think this was the bit I was more excited about! Not actually going out in it, but just the event of buying it! I ordered a few bits and pieces from Missguided online, in sizes 10 and (fingers crossed) a size 8 too, with the hope this would be my first ever size 8 dress to celebrate the three-zero mark! And sure enough, it was!

I was amazed as I stood in it and slowly but surely did up the zip, yep all the way to the top! I think I squealed out loud and just stood there in it looking in the new full lengthen mirror I had ever owned in my entire life. *This literally can't be true, can it?* I thought to myself. It must be a big size 8, stretchy fabric or something, surely…but whatever it was, I couldn't quite believe it, it was so surreal, I had to pinch myself, really hard this time! I don't think I had ever, in my entire life, fitted in to a size 8. Not even as an 11- or 12-year-old girl. I remember jumping right in to an adult size 14 when I hit those teenage years…this, to me, was one of the best birthday presents I could have ever given myself. Or anyone could have given me for that matter.

As I got ready on the night of my birthday, again, I couldn't quite believe this was my birthday outfit; it may seem so silly to some people, but this really was one of the biggest non-scale victories I had throughout in my journey. Not saying that a size 8 is what we should wish for, it was just an occasion I never thought would be possible just a few years earlier for myself. Me fitting in to a LBD for my 30th birthday. The best bit of all was that I felt absolutely amazing, not just how I looked, but on the inside too, I was truly happy and healthy and it showed!

I actually did really enjoy the night out with three of my amazing girlfriends and it was a lovely evening, not too wild, as you know me the not-so-big-party-animal those days, but just a nice night to mark the event, and I am really glad I did something to celebrate! But more so that I could say I was as healthy and as fit as I could have possibly have been the day I turned 30! What a gift to myself!

The weeks following drew us closer to the Christmas festive weeks, and New Year's Eve, which that year was fairly similar to my thought process before my birthday. I had enough big wild trashy nights out in my past, to not be too fussed by one more NYE. So, I spent it with my best friend Cheryl, with a few others at a house gathering local to where we lived, seeing in the new year, only having one sip of champagne to years everyone as the clock stuck midnight, then I was quite happy to call it a night shortly after the 12:00 A.M. fireworks and everyone had said their well wishes, hugs and kisses all round, I was ready to head home! (I know, I know…bag of fun, I was! LOL!)

It's just my life had changed so much, and my priorities too. In fact, the next morning, I was marking New Year's Day with a massive group workout, myself, Charles and another friend Lydia had organised to celebrate the first day of the year in a healthier way, without 25–30 of friends getting in a massive communal gym session at Legends Gym in Haringey, North London. Gone were the days of only a few years ago, spending New Year's Day in bed nursing an incredibly bad hangover, feeling sorry for myself! Not anymore, I would be feeling fit and fresh as a daisy tomorrow, and the best bit was I was looking forward to it I couldn't wait to wake up already and I hadn't even gone to sleep yet!

I actually didn't enjoy being out partying that much, whilst I knew my time could be better spent elsewhere. There was so much I wanted to achieve and it seemed my big future plans all rested on this weight loss journey and writing the book that I believed could really catapult all my dreams, ideas and business plans to follow in to reality.

I vowed to myself that night, not just as any old new year's resolution to mark the beginning of a new year, but as a real life commitment that I didn't care if it took me 2, 5, 10 years, I was going to see out every business idea I'd been visualising in my brain that I wanted to achieve, inspired from my change in lifestyle and weight loss, and I decided I really wanted to turn this passion into something special—a whole empire in fact! I wanted to make my passion my pay check, so that is exactly what I began to plan out! Bring on 2016!

Chapter 24
D-Day: The Two-Year Mark

It was fast approaching last day of February 2016, the day that would mark the phenomenal two years since I woke up that cold and rainy day in 2014 with the dreaded pins and needles that triggered my lifestyle change. This was it! The goal I had set myself, and more importantly, the deadline, the final prize, almost 24 months earlier.

I was pushing myself everyday as the time drew closer, still going for that goal, and with all the anticipation, everything I had worked for to get me to this point. It had been building up over the two years all the way to this very day, I couldn't quite believe it, I was almost there, the finish line in sight! Would I make it, would I hit my goal? What if I didn't? No, that was not an option…doubt is never an option I thought as I grinned to myself!

I worked so hard for this. Too damn hard for myself! *Look at how far you've come,* I thought, *two whole years! Every day you have got up and done this with the biggest smile on your face, knowing what it meant to you, never giving up, never looking back and never falling off that wagon, Carli!* I said pep-talking to myself.

Then finally, it was really here. The 29th of February 2016, arrived with excitement and anxious feelings all at once as I woke that morning. Realising instantly how different I felt compared to the paralysed feeling that had rudely woken me up back in 2014 shocking me in to action and ultimately a new life. *Wow,* I thought to myself, *feel the difference, look at you, take it all in! What a journey this has been! Girl! You made it…* and as I weighed myself that day, I saw I really had! I'd done it! Shed half my body weight in 24 months like I had planned, vowed, promised to myself! All by myself too! No help from anyone, just little ole me!

The feeling was immense, it's hard to explain it, a mixture of emotions: accomplishment, satisfaction, happiness and quite frankly just proud! I couldn't believe it, I literally felt like I'd lost half of me, but gained twice the life! And in hindsight, I really had when you thought about it.

This was all so odd, so surreal still (again pinching myself), from being the overweight obese girl majority of my life, over a quarter of a century living that way, on average wearing UK size 20–24 clothes to now this! Whoever would have thought…but as they say, thoughts do become things if you want it and work for it bad enough!

If you had of asked me 4–5 years back if I would ever be a size 8–10, I would have laughed in your face, as my arm could barely fit in to a size 8 trouser leg, let alone my leg. But this was it, I had done it.

Even though I had reached this goal, this was a lifestyle now, it wasn't the end, it wasn't over, no, if anything this was just the beginning. No time to waste and no time to spare, I was at my peak.

I marked the occasion, more so with just that euphoric feeling of knowing what I had accomplished in two years, that was all a reward in itself! I was proud of myself, and not just the physical weight loss, but the whole 360 lifestyle change, finding my passion, and most importantly, finding me and what I wanted to do with my life going forward! This had really proved to me I could take control of every outcome in my life and make my life what I truly wanted it to be! There was no stopping what I was capable of now.

I took note of the occasion, honoured the day as a victory to me and as the anniversary of my best self and then that was that, roll on the new month of March!

I, now, just wanted to keep it up: be the best, fittest, healthiest version of me I could become. It's like I went in to overdrive a bit, spending every waking moment working out, attending more and more body building gyms all over London, meeting other fitness enthusiasts, and pretty much exercising all weekend at gyms all over the city including MuscleWorks Gym in Bethnal Green, Legends Gym in Haringey or Metroflex in Sydenham, alongside my local PureGym during the week as this is what I enjoyed doing in my free time. I just couldn't stop, it was a full blown hobby, passion and life for me now, and I was loving it!

****

But as the days passed and into the next month I went, I couldn't help but feel, was that it, the big hoo-rah I was expecting?! *You have hit your goal, Carli,* I thought...and yes, don't get me wrong, I was damn proud of what I had set out to achieve, don't get that twisted, but I guess like winning a race or coming first in a contest or marathon, that's it, you've done it, it's over. But this goal and subsequently, the lifestyle and body was far from over for me, there was no finish line so to speak. Maybe not fully comprehending it back then at the time, but eventually, realising it over the coming weeks and months, post-goal, that this is the one race, the one competition you enter and embark on in life, for life! That the finish line keeps getting further and further away, like a never-ending race really.

Now, take it from me that this may seem to some people like the most awful running race you've ever entered, but I can tell you now, it's not, this is just the beginning, the first hurdle or high jump so to speak, and it's all about to get even better. Do not stop now.

Just know, if you get to this point in your journey and you realise what I realised, seeing it as a positive thing, and you keep on going, this is the point your life will change to an even greater state! As I truly believe this is where 95% of people fail! They achieve their first weight loss goal and then stop, kaput, finale! Thinking they've done it, got the results they wanted and now they don't have to do anything to keep them, the results will stay, and then that's when so many people pile all the weight back on that they have just spent so much time, and effort losing.

But I think if that 95% of people saw it as a lifestyle, changed their outlook, their way of thinking and working, adopting a better mental process, and embrace it as more a healthy fitter way of life, enjoying the full process and journey, rather than just a weight loss goal with an ending, then we wouldn't see so many people putting the weight back on after they achieved what they always wanted. Like someone handing you a million dollars, then taking it off you the next day.

Instead, you want to be the 5% that succeed past their initial goal and live on to tell of the aftermath and their success. If you want that, then ask yourself are you ready? I mean really ready for it? If the answer is yes, then here we go, keep those running shoes firmly fastened, the real race is just about to start. And you are the only competitor. Here we go, babyyy!

Chapter 25
Okay, So You Made It!

So as I said, the last chapter was the big sha-bang! Well done, Hooray! You did it! And yes, let's re-cap that, I really had done it, and don't get me wrong, I really was proud of what I had achieved! I'm quite hard on myself sometimes and always wanting more, as I know what I am capable of, and always one for pushing on forward. I never ever settle, because if I achieve one thing, then I think what's next? It gets my gears going, you know. As I know there is always more with me! More, more, more!

I came to realise the months following during 2016, following my goal point of losing half my body weight, that it was like this lull, a what to do now period? Everyone talks about setting goals, wanting to lose weight, getting that desired body, but what do you do when you get there?

No one really talks about the plan once you get there, and what to do to make the results last forever, and hence, why I think so many people put the weight back on, or don't even want to start in the first place, as the journey ahead looks hard, or impossible. Yes, we hear it all the time, people saying you have to maintain it, but what does that really mean, that's common sense, but how do you actually do that, and really maintain the results you have just got?

So, I'm going to address it based on my experience, the good, the bad, the unexpected and most importantly, the tactics and solutions to make the most of your hard work and keep that goal alive and getting even more from your results!

Don't be the stereotype yo-yo dieter. "Oh yeah, but she's put it all back on now, and more…" Be the 'she lost so much weight and kept it off' type!

But this is the bit everyone forgets, it's not over, but some think it is. They reward themselves with a big meal, girl's night out on the vino, or a dessert to say, "Great, I hit my weight-loss goal, I'm done now, I can eat again." Wrong. So wrong. Remember, don't reward yourself with food!

This to me says you didn't do it the right way in the first place, you missed the point of making it a lifestyle, you didn't enjoy the process, you were just doing it for a one time only goal, and now, you're going to put it all back on and potentially more. You didn't do it for life, for you, for the long haul.

You fell back in to what majority of the want-to-lose-weight population does, you did it for a short-term goal, quick beach body, holiday is coming up, wedding on the horizon etc…you didn't do it for your life. You didn't get rid of your bad habits.

I'm not wanting to sound harsh, I just don't sugar coat anything (not even my food these days LOL). If you know me from my posts on Instagram, or like my friends know me in real life, I'm very, very direct, I say it how it is, I'm raw with my words and I speak in real terms. I speak the truth, even if it hurts to hear, because you know it's true. But sometimes, that's the only way to really make a change. Be honest with yourself.

So, here is where I really want to address these issues, and if you've made it this far in my book, not getting too bored of my nonsense rambling, then I promise you there is something inside you that wants this journey and goal to work for you this final time; you want to give weight loss one last shot and for it to stick for life. No more fads, no more giving up, no more gimmicks! No more starting over each time, you want this now! If you truly believe it, you are half way there with the right mind-set with the new thinking of 'Getting healthy, fit and then losing weight.'

I want to address the most important thing in a mass weight loss journey, the point just after the goal is hit—the MAINTENANCE! To what most people seems straight forward: "Oh yeah, I'll just now keep it off now, I've done it."

I think this bit is actually more difficult than the initial weight loss itself IF you don't plan for it. Hence, why, yes, I was excited at my two year mark of hitting my goal, but I knew it wasn't over. This was the important bit if I wanted to hold on to my prize, my trophy, the new me for life.

Just like any sport, course, studying you do, you train yourself, you do research, you revise, you test yourself, you go over and over your notes, drilling in to your mind all the facts, what you've learnt so when you sit the test to pass, you get that A or 100% mark…

I treat weight loss as the same, we have to study for it, prepare our minds and body, just like any sport, to get better and better each month as they pass. A footballer or a Gymnast practises and trains for years to get better, healthier, fitter at their sport. You are no different with what you are trying to learn or train yourself for. Now, to some people that may seem stupid, sports and athletes are so different to people wanting to lose weight. And yes, the physical chosen sport may be different, but yet, it's the mind-set, dedication, willingness to preserver, work hard to be the best at their game and that is the same for anyone wanting to achieve any type of goal in life and be the best at their own game!

Chapter 26
Maintaining 101

As you creep steadily towards your goal that you've set for yourself, over whatever time frame you thought was reasonable, imagine the feeling of getting there. Yep, all the way to the end, achieving that very thing!

I'm sure it's a vision, dream, or wish you've had etched in your mind for a while now, so you know exactly what it is and how it looks. The image could be of a slimmer you, or maybe more muscular, a flatter stomach, slender arms, perkier butt, or maybe it's to run a half marathon, or squat 100 kg...whatever it is, the vision will look different for everyone, depending on what it is you are seeking out as your overall goal for your healthier, fitter version of yourself!

Imaging what you would look like having achieved this goal, how you would feel once that becomes reality, how people will react to your new look or accomplishment, what clothes you will buy, imagine how you feel on the inside, how healthy fit and focused you can be, less stress and anxiety, what more you can achieve with the better version of you, what other sports you can now try, what your new found health can do for you?? Yes, imagine all of this!

Now, us humans have this tendency to self-sabotage, especially just before we succeed! It's like the evil twin on our left shoulder trying to test us, see if we are really ready and wanting this goal to come true! I've had it, we all have at some point in our life! It could be just before your weigh day, or when you've had good results, or right before the final goal, and then you just go fuck it all up for yourself, knowing full well what you are doing!

STOP this! Stop this right now, this is the most important time to dig deep for that willpower, kick your strong mind in to gear. YOU WILL SUCEED! Nothing is going to stop you this time.

You have full power to control this little devil, obstacle, sabotage...whatever you want to call it, it's a test, don't give in to it! You are stronger than that and your goal is worth more than that little moment of temptation, trying one last time to pull you off course.

So, again, imagine your goal, body, the feeling and choose something special to do for yourself to mark that achievement when you get there. This shouldn't have to involve a big night out drinking, eating crappy food or doing something the old bigger or unhealthier you would do to celebrate—this is to celebrate the new YOU—the better, healthier fitter you!

Choose a reward like an activity you will remember, something you've always wanted to do your entire life, or a pamper day, or perhaps it's an outfit that once upon a time you never would have dreamed you could fit in to. Just choose something to mark the occasion of your new image and overall feeling that once was a vision, because it will now be real.

Then put in small incremental milestones and measure points to get you to the final stages and that ultimate goal. Take pictures and body measurements along the way to see your progress to keep you motivated that you are changing, no matter how small the change may be, you are getting somewhere. Be realistic with these goals and timeframes and don't rush them, otherwise you are just setting yourself up for failure. Be reasonable, pushing yourself fairly, and each time you reach one of the mini goals in-between, this will spur you on to keep going, instead of setting unrealistic goals you don't reach and then want to quit. You need to work with yourself here! Be your own support.

During the journey and the months that pass, enjoy every moment of the process, appreciate what you can do, and most importantly, love yourself a little more because this is you and your body, we only get one and you really have to love the skin you're in to become that ultimate best you.

As you get there, be proud, be happy and most of all know what you have sacrificed to get here, know you have put in all the hard work you could, and you've done it for you, learning more about yourself than you ever would dieting, detoxing, 'fading' your life away.

The day you get there, celebrate, in a healthy way, enjoy it! And yes, have a day or two off, or hey, maybe you even take a week to enjoy yourself within reason—don't blow it though! Know your own strengths and weaknesses that come with a break. I know your friends and family will say, "Oh, let your hair down, you've earned it, you've been so good, you've done it now!" But this is the critical week, the week post-big goal triumph, hence why you need to prep your present and reward to yourself in advance, something significant to mark it.

This week is the time some people go 100% backwards and the point of no return for some after all the hard work and effort they have put in to get here. Now, you will know your own willpower by now through your journey, and even the strongest of mind-set can do a 180 back to their old selves real quick like you wouldn't believe. Don't let that be you. You know yourself know. That's what this whole body and health transformation has been about.

I'm not trying to scare you or say don't enjoy yourself, again this is me just being real! Do enjoy yourself, just enjoy yourself in the right way. We are not out on a hen-do or stag, partying the life away we have just earned! You don't win a billion dollars and then chuck it all away!

Now, a few days post reward and hitting your big goal, I want you to look at old photos, old you, pre-healthy days, and old clothes that are now too big for you. Really take in what you have achieved, savour the comments from people, put on a new item of clothing, sit and look in the mirror, see what you have done and note how good you feel inside and out! Remember this moment! Be proud, you really have done so well!

Now, at the end of this book, I've made a section for you all to use to write your initial goals, achievements and summaries. So, once you've got to your goal and this maintenance stage (because you will make it there this time), take out a pen and I want you to write on there 3–5 things you love about the new you. It may be the way you look, what you now can do, the way you think, the weight you lost, your determination, fitness PB's you smashed along the way, anything! Just write what YOU love about YOU. Then I want you to write 3–5 things about how those new qualities and achievements are going to help you achieve your next new life goals! So, then, of course, write what those 1–2 new goals are! Now, these can be weight related again, further improvements, new sports you want to try, a new dress size, something ticked off the bucket list, an action-packed activity, adding muscle mass, something the previous you couldn't do or didn't have. BUT now you know you will AND can do, without question! Because simply you have the ability to achieve anything you set your mind to!

Make these realistic, with a suitable time frame around them again, and then without further-a-do, get to it! Again, start small working on your new goals, as it will give you something to work towards and keep you in the new healthy lifestyle and mind-set, going forwards, not backwards post-goal!

With maintenance, people get there and slip back to the old them, reverting to old habits that weren't quite erased rather just hidden. With nothing to work for and no new goals, old habits can come back, so don't be that person!

You are a new person, you have the ability, willpower, strength and body you have always wanted, don't waste it, use it now to be even better, go beyond, on to the next level! The most amazing tool you will ever have, your body—and God only granted you one—don't give up now. The lifestyle you have created is just beginning, embrace it! This is where the 1% of people succeed and go on to do even great things, so be part of that statistic and let's help it grow beyond a single percentile.

Chapter 27
Be Prepared: Temptations, Cravings and Relapses

Now, it all seems so simple right, well, yes, in theory, but again, there are going to be hurdles, bumps and mishaps along the way as the journey continues. But this time round, you are stronger in mind and body, you've learnt about yourself, your pitfalls, your weaknesses and strengths.

Everything you now know from round one, on your way to the first goal, you should be well-aware of your traits now and see them coming, you are ahead of yourself now, and can pre-empt and pre-plan things as you know how your body reacts, your triggers and how much willpower you have and when to use it.

A lot of the time it can be emotional triggers, situations, feelings or people that come up in our lives that can set even the most determined person back. So, what I'm saying is be prepared that they will occur at some point; it's reality, as we don't always know what's around the corner in life and what is going to get thrown at us. Just know you are not alone, things are going to come up in life, that may make you want to recluse to the old you, the comfort zone you knew for so, so long, the emotional eating binge phases, drinking, having just one cigarette, whatever it may be, it's an urge to just go wild and off the rails to a life you once knew for a long period of your life. Is that worth it to you? Whatever, it might be, life is going to go on and you need to try stay in your strongest mental state through these times, this is the new health fit you who is mentally capable of dealing with any situation! You will get through it, without giving it to temptations, they will not help you.

Depending on the life woe that may come your way, depends on how much willpower and self-motivation you are going to have to dig deep for, so keep those goals you wrote down earlier close by and keep old photos at the ready, knowing you are a stronger you now, in more ways than one! You've got this!

The reason I say this above as a pre-warning is yes, it all happened to me too! It's like I've been a guinea-pig testing out my theories in order to be able to write about my experiences and in some way, guide you as to what I went through, and what you may too. Then being able to shed some light on how I over-came the situations, as to get the best results, so in turn you can as well, no matter what life throws at you.

So, with all that in mind, I set out to put my new theories and ways in to practise in 2016 post-two year mark. Bearing in mind this was all new to me too, a new way of thinking, a path I had never been done before. A path post success for once.

Old Carli had, too, tried all the weird and whacky fads on the market during my late teens and early 20s actually trying to losing weight the right way. But this was my first time that I had successfully committed to doing it right, so we are in this together! Hence why it took me so long to actually write this book, I could have just finished this book when I hit my goal and the big shebang and be done with it. But I wanted to share beyond that and as I had to see how I did 1–2 years on from my goal weight in order to be able to write all about it and tell you if my theories and methods actually did work for me, and keeping the weight off for the long haul.

There were hard times past my initial goal that I could have fallen off the wagon so to speak, piled the weight back on, joining so many out there who can't keep the weight off. But that's what old Carli would have done. Not this time! This time round, I was stronger mentally and physically! I had taken 24 months to get to know myself and how I worked, and responded, and that's why doing the long-haul way, I think is beneficially and gives more success than any diet out there. It's more than just losing weight, it's a learning curve, a lifestyle change, a journey and a process of really getting to know yourself better than anyone else ever will.

There is no obstacle or hurdle that can stand in your way as you push on throughout your healthy life. You cannot fail this time round.

So yes, there were scenarios throughout 2016, let's call them 'distractions', that came along, whether it be in the form of a partner and dating, certain friend scenarios, family issues or work occasions and stress, that could have brought me down, unfocused me, distracted me from where I was heading (and some of them did for a month or so, not completely but just took some of my attention and energy away from myself and goals) trying to pull me back in to old ways I had known oh so well once pun a time, but this time, I knew what I had achieved was too great to let anything pull me away completely from where I was heading.

You have to always look at the overall prize and bigger picture and think about what is more important? Your health and life or worrying over little everyday scenarios that may come up. Always keep the focus on you and what it is that you want and what really makes you happy going forward. Know when to walk away, as not everyone or thing you lose is a loss. Remember that!

During any of these encounters above, you may go through a rough patch, for example let's say with a partner, and feel like emotionally eating, binging, and cravings start to come back up, and you so desperately want that item of food, especially sugar, one of the worst addictions of all that so many people can relate to. Once you have that taste for it, even the tiniest bit, it can get you back in to a bad cycle and start to unravel all the work you've done. Don't let feelings fail you.

You really have to install a methodology with yourself; is the want and taste of a craving now that may last 2–3 minutes really, really worth ruining your overall long-term goal for? Think about which one is more important? That piece of cake or chocolate now? Or the healthy life and body you've wanted for so long?

Some people may think 'oh, but it's just one piece?' But is it really? Now, yes, some people out there can just have one piece, but we all know majority of us can't just have one bit of chocolate, or one biscuit, a thin slice of cake etc…the whole pack is gone before we know it, our taste buds go crazy, possess us, taking over…for real! I know I've been there and devoured boxes of biscuits equalling over 2,000 calories in one go, with the intention to just have one.

I do think for people who have been morbidly obese and severely overweight for majority of their life deal with overcoming food issues and weight loss on a different level than say someone that may have been slimmer or within a healthier BMI for most of their life and then for example hit their 30s or 40s and packed on some extra weight, or for instance a slim mum trying to lose post-baby weight. Everyone's weight loss goals or issues will have different methods to combat them, some easier than others.

At the end of the day, it's about knowing your limits and is it worth it, to you, the individual, and your overall situation? Maybe yes, you've had a good week and allowed a treat meal, I'm not saying don't have anything, just know what is right for you, your limits and how you react to certain food groups, alongside the mood and mental state you are in that day. Basically, be more self-aware of your emotional well-being and feelings.

These crazy cravings often stem from our bodies actually craving certain nutrients. It actually may be something our body is lacking, like magnesium, or Vitamin B etc...there are a whole range of them, but our bodies scream out for them in cravings we can mistake for sugar or salts, and then we can't stop thinking about them until we have the item we associate our craving with.

This can be due to the reward hormone in our bodies called Dopamine. Dopamine remembers how sugars or salts make us feel with food addictions. Dopamine works the same with any type of addict: drugs, alcohol, sex, even people addicted to using their phones, social media, gambling etc...

Dopamine remembers the good feelings these items give us instantly, sending a reward signal to the brain, so when we are down, emotional, or craving this 'bad' thing, Dopamine remembers the sudden satisfaction we get from that 'bad' item, making us want it this very instant like a drug. However, dopamine does not register or remember the guilt we feel afterwards. The regret, remorse, the disappointment...nope, Dopamine only remembers the instant hit and good signal our brain is receiving when we give in to that item.

Remember that next time you have a craving for anything bad, its Dopamine wanting the bad stimulant you used to satisfy your urges with, your brain remembers that thought and feeling only. It's usually a good indication if you know that last time you had this item you felt really bad after, and you know you will regret it. Try to let that thought have control over the dopamine in the brain.

You need to try and re-train or trick your dopamine hormone. Feeling real satisfaction from new 'better-for-you' items, so in turn, we crave these new items. It can work, I have managed to replace old cravings and items of food, with new healthier options, and on occasion, I actually find myself craving nuts and dried fruit when I go to the movies instead of popcorn and lollies. I've even found myself craving fresh blended green juices over hot chocolates and sugary drinks... I know it sounds odd, but they really can hit the spot, you just have to take control over your own mind and in such the dopamine in your body.

Make a list of all your bad triggers and foods, and find suitable substitutes for days where you feel it's not a 'treat' day or some days are worse than others, you may be emotional, facing things that day in life that you are not as strong as other days. These occasions need substitute foods to keep you at bay! It won't happen overnight, but over time, your taste buds, cravings, brain signals and yes, that good old Dopamine will change. When you eat these new good foods, really enjoy the taste and tell yourself how good they are making you feel on the inside and out. Savour that thought.

I'm saying this because there are times you will just want to chuck it all in and binge, or have out-of-control urges for sugar and countless amounts of food even though you may not actually be hungry. This could be because of something going on in your life at a certain time, and I know this because there were one to two times I can recount a full-on food sugar binge where it's like something had come over me. Yes, old-big-Carli was trying to come out.

Chapter 28
Addiction and Binges

I was at a friend's wedding, and even though I felt like I was physically and mentally strong all the time, a very small event or scenario can trigger mood or feelings. If I was at home, I think I may have not done this, but then when in a scenario faced with old foods, drink, and partying, in an environment I didn't know so well anymore, I reacted differently to what I thought I would have. I was caught off guard by my own actions.

I'd had a bad day and an argument with someone I was dating at the time. They'd really pissed me off and I had a bad feeling of anxiety coming over me. The whole situation had been playing on my mind the whole time I was at this wedding, I couldn't stop thinking about it, almost winding myself up (you know how us girls do, playing over and over the scenario in your head, thinking of all the outcomes…yeah, one of those ones situations…)

During the reception as the wedding cake arrived, I contemplated not even having a slice, but then thought, I've been good, I can control myself; why not just have a small slice? So, I did. But that little taste of processed sugar, all the sweetness, fats and processed carbs that my taste buds weren't really used to anymore as my diet and daily food intake had changed so much hit me all at once! My dopamine, taste buds, insulin levels and cravings went in to overdrive; it's like my mouth was having a party of its own, reminiscing this flavour it hadn't had in so long!

I went back for seconds without even thinking about it grabbing a bigger slice this time, literally just hovering near the cake tray, eating without it even touching the sides of my mouth, swallowing before it had even been chewed! Then my hand was going in for another and another…before my willpower eventually decided to wake the hell up, kicking in to gear scream at me, "Carli, WHAT the fuck are you doing? Who are you right now?!"

I was appalled and shocked at myself?!? How many calories had I just devoured in like the space of three minutes…surely, it was about 2,000! Anyone would think I was a starving child who hadn't seen food for 30 days. I had scoffed down more cake than I had possibly had in over a year, like on autopilot hand-to-mouth on repeat.

I've never been someone to ever be bulimic, or even think about throwing up food after eating it, I didn't have that in me to ever do, but at that moment, I literally wanted to, but of course, I would never do that, but the thought to want to get the food out of me was enough.

I realised I could so have slipped back in to old ways. It was then that I realised our feelings and emotions really can betray us, if we let them. Emotional eating,

111

eating out of habit or boredom can creep back in so easily. I knew I couldn't let my guard down again. I had to take action and not let scenarios and hurdles in my life take effect over my goals and plans for myself, my health and my life. That argument with the guy I was seeing was definitely not a priority over my body and hard work. It's not like he was my long-term partner or husband, the argument was irrelevant, he wasn't worth it and I shouldn't have even cared, as it's all a distant memory now and so insignificant.

Yes, I know a few slices of cake didn't actually ruin everything, and it was a once in blue moon occasion, but it was more the way I went about it, hoovering it down like I was unconscious! Believe me, I could have kept eating it if I hadn't of stopped myself. The poor bride may not have even got a slice of her own cake, she may have had to fight me for it, literally! LOL!

Jokes aside, I really could have had 6, 8, 10+ slices! I could eat without feeling full or sick still, like a bottomless pit. That was more the scary thing, that 127 kg Carli could have come back. I know albeit only this one occasion but that was enough for me. The cake in that three minutes was not worth going backwards for.

This is what I meant about knowing your limits each day and state of mind. If I know I cannot control myself just to have one slice, one piece, one item of food, than I go without that day. Don't get me wrong, there have been days in the office where someone brings in cake and I can have a tiny piece and walk away.

But I know self-control and endless calories can still be a problem thing for me, so, I have to know what I'm playing with each day, we are all human, but I've worked too hard to let too many of those food binges happen.

As for me, that one day of eating endless cake, could have turned in to two days off, a week off…and there it goes… I would entered the population of people that go backwards…it really can happen that easily from one big binge. Like people say, don't let one cheat meal turn in to a cheat week.

Eventually, shortly after my cake episode, I left the wedding. I wasn't going to be staying late anyways, and had planned to be at the gym the next morning as part of my normal routine, and now I knew that would definitely have to happen! I had extra miles to churn on that bike after all that cake! I wasn't too hard on myself, I knew situations like that mishap could occur with anyone, that's part of being human and it could have been worse, but what I did know about myself was that I had to take control of it early. Not let it keep going, and gaining a bad habit, you have to kill those off real quick. Sometimes, removing myself from a scenario is the best way—out of sight, out of mind.

The worst part about it was I don't think I even liked the cake taste and flavour that much anyways, I think it was chocolate, but it literally was the sugar, icing and cream filling that my taste buds used to love too much and went crazy for.

I know, to this day, I still have a bad sugar and food addiction; it always was one of my worst habits growing up, a sweet tooth alongside the ability to consume endless amounts of calories without feeling full. For me, I know these were and always will be my worst two things I have to keep an eye on! Even today, I am conscious of eating too many calories, even of health foods like salads, nuts, avocados, yogurts and even natural sugars in dried fruits, mangos, cherries etc…of course, I know these are better for me, but I could sit and eat an entire packet of dates in one minute flat! That's talent, I hear some of you say, and if anyone ever needs me to enter one of those food eating competitions of how much you can devour in 60 seconds, yeah, I'm your woman! LOL! Moderation, my dear girl, moderation!

For everyone, it will be a different trigger. I know for some of my friends it's biscuits, or crisps and chips, others it's glasses of wine or cigarettes, we all have something a life trigger can send us sky-rocketing for, so know your emotional state and willpower each and every single day, and don't be caught off guard!

****

This is a diary extract I wrote in October 2016, shortly after the wedding scenario, I realised I really had been battling an addiction.

I've suddenly realised I was, correction I am, really addicted to food. Not like people joking around saying addicted to chocolate. But I realised I'm scared of being hungry, like I generally fear being without food or not being able to get hold of some. I'm sitting on this train right now and literally have enough food with me for the day, but a bit extra 'in case' I need some.

Now, I know this can also be seen as meal prep to some people, but I don't have the extra food with me to stop me snacking or buying other stuff it's in case I get hungry and can't get out to get more food if I'm in the office or in a meeting at work.

It's only just hit me. I generally have just realised I actually fear being hungry, like I'll go in to a state or panic if, for one second, I feel hunger and can't eat. It's like I'm a drug addict, and finished my last stash, and fear not being able to score again.

The thought of being overly full is natural to me and does not give me the sick feeling anymore others may get when over eating, but the thought of even being hungry scares me, even thinking about it gives me slight anxiety right now. As I comprehend this all now and the realisation has come to me that I honestly can't remember the last time I was genuinely hungry or that feeling of being ravenous or starving. Because I simply don't let myself get to that state, I'm constantly eating.

Now, I know it is good to eat small meals often like I try to do to speed up my metabolism, but it's about balancing the two, and not eating for the sake of it. I really needed to think, 'Am I actually hungry right now, do I need to eat, or is it habit?'

It's like I constantly still need to be chewing or sipping on something to feel content, even if it's healthy food. Now, I know I have always loved food, but I've just realised I am really battling a very long addiction with the need for food 24/7. Even currently, with 'better option' foods, 21 months in to my weight loss journey.

Breaking my 30 year want for constant food is tough and will continue to do so. It's like people with cigarettes, alcohol, drugs, gambling or sugar. It's comfort, you enjoy it, it makes you feel good, and then bad, then regret, then back to want again (thinking you need it) but you don't, you will survive and be better off without it.

So, now that I have realised I have been truly addicted to food, how am I going to overcome this? As I think this solution will be what helps me lose my weight and get to my overall goal.

At the end of the day, self-realisation, self-acknowledgement and of course self-motivation is what will get you through. Knowing you don't need these things constantly to live your life, that you can live an adjustment of them is what I need to do now. I know it, it's just putting it in to action.

It's like my taste buds always needed that fix, and when they get it, any kind of food, it just wants more, more, more!! Sometimes, I wish I never had taste buds, honestly, there are days I could really do without them!

They crave food all day long, I literally am always thinking about what I'm going to eat, and then the fact that I need it now, I can't function or think about anything else until I get it. Like the urge is so strong, and when I get it, it's like my whole body is satisfied and I could have ten times what I've just eaten.

I know people joke about food ruling their life, but I truly believe it has for me for long. I'm going away for work next week for five days and my first thought was what am I going to eat, will I have enough food with me, what if I get hungry? Honestly, I can't believe I'm thinking like that. What if I can't get my hands-on food when I need it?

A lot of people say they combat one addiction with another to compensate and maybe that is what I am doing with my endless hours of exercise (although I actually do enjoy the exercise, it's not forced), but at least that's a good action to have! But I really need to combat the food one. Writing this is somehow making it better, like being honest with myself. I knew I always loved food but when you physically fear and panic being without it, that is a problem.

I fear being in the car, stuck in traffic and being hungry, and that could only be four miles from home, not far at all, but I fear being stuck in that situation. Some people may read this and think it sounds so stupid and not be able to understand it, but it's the same with sugar, amphetamines or alcohol addiction.

Food addiction is real, the ability to consume endless calories with no feeling of too much, simply not enough, is what some people like me, go through. People don't always identify it as a true addiction, like I have just done at age 30, even months in to my weight loss journey, I've just identified one of my biggest issues with food, as a real actual problem, so here's hoping what has been a fairly easy journey for me so far, with my willpower and determination, that this could now become even easier that I've identified this thought process around food and one of my biggest issues and bad habits as an actual addiction.

I know this will always be key to success with any goal, identifying problems, realising them, analyse them, finding solutions to combat them and then put those changes in to practise to solve them and rid yourself of the problem at altogether! Instead of letting this be a stumbling point where you give up, you have to face them head on and address them.

Food addiction can be one of the worst things to be addicted to, I think, as the majority of society doesn't categorise it or see it as a real addiction and issue, some will probably laugh at the fact and ridicule the thought saying, 'shut up, you're just fat!'. But there is no public help for it like drug or alcohol addiction from the health services. So, in hindsight, it's not treated as an addiction, but simply people that just over eat! But today, I've decided I would do something about it and treat it like any other addiction, and help myself overcome it!

Chapter 29
The Only Way Is Up

OK, so back on track and moving in the only direction I knew possible: forward. Despite that one little encounter with the cake, it wasn't the be all and end all of my journey. Hell no, I'd come too far to only come this far.

I just had to write about it and share it with you all as some people get really down on themselves with scenarios like that, but you are not alone, and it doesn't have to take over everything. This does not mean you've fallen off the wagon, and have to give up, thinking you've ruined everything. Look at scenarios that happen, analyse it, how you reacted, acknowledge what's happened, and overcome it. Don't let it linger on in to the next day. It's about how you pick yourself back up and what you take from it. Another lesson to add to your mental checklist of triggers, woes, or weaknesses that you can be aware of and find a solution to overcome, so next time, it's a different outcome.

There were many scenarios that happened to me during 2016 that could have pulled me off track, got me down, but I knew I was a fighter and always had been so headstrong, that there was nothing worth giving all this up for. Especially not over some minor man drama. Please. Ain't no one got time for that shit.

I had a busy year with work, managing various clients, projects and recruitment campaigns across the UK and various locations, even travelling to Angola and Germany on occasions and still having to maintain my healthy eating and exercise. There was no excuse for me, I had to keep at it. My hours were all over the place and I was still trying to keep at my routine, finding time for the gym where ever I was in the world and prepping my food in advance so that was one less thing to think about when back home in the UK. Lucky enough for me, being organised and structured comes naturally, and it's a great characteristic to have as it really aids in you sticking to the plan, and there are no temptations to grab food on the go when you're extra busy. I think that's the quick and easy option, 'cause it ain't always what's best for you!

I had to also keep reminding myself that this is my lifestyle now that I had chosen and committed to, embracing it every day, as it was far better than the way of life I used to live. No one could argue with that, that's for sure. I knew this from the way I felt every morning I woke up, alive, healthy, full of energy and fit!

Along with really embedding my new ways in everyday life and responsibilities, not slipping backwards, learning to maintain what I had achieved, setting this as my new routine, and practising good habits, there were also a lot of good things happening at the time. These kept me on track, proud of what I had achieved and my inner motivation bubbling away.

I was approached by a journalist from a national press company to work with me writing an editorial of my story to pitch to the national papers and women's magazines to share my story, to which it was picked up by Bella magazine, Real Life and The Sun here in the UK, as well as the Huffington Post Australia, US and UK, Daily Mail Australia and That's Life Magazine.

I was so excited, it felt great to be able to share my story past Instagram, and the response was great, from people all over the world saying they had seen my articles, from old friends who barely recognised me to complete strangers in remote towns who had become new followers and supporters.

By far, the Sun was one of my favourite experiences from all these articles, getting picked up in this beautiful black Mercedes with a chauffeur at Waterloo and taken to the News UK building at London Bridge. I had a great afternoon with the team: a stylist Siobhan, make-up and hair artist Elouise, photographer Stew and his assistant Marie. They were all so great, making my first ever photo shoot for the paper feel so natural and comfortable, I just loved every minute of it, and it gave me a real taste for what I wanted to do going forward. I'll always be thankful to all the team that day and the journalist Jenny, for running my story and the whole overall experience. It really made me want to keep doing what I was doing, and it instilled an even further urge for me to want to pursue this all as a career.

I could feel I was really starting to get somewhere with all of this, and it wasn't just about my weight loss anymore, it was more than that. I wanted to turn this in to something bigger and better, something that any person could take something away from my story; no matter what your life goal or ambition was, that you could achieve what you set out to do in life!

Now, for most of who follow me, it could be weight loss, health, muscle gain, or any sort of body transformation goal, but for some, it could be going for something in life you've always wanted—having your dream job, travelling across the world, starting your own business, learning a new skill or sport. Just taking any dream or wish, and turning it in to a reality was what I wanted to help inspire people to do! I wanted to instil in people that they really could have whatever they wanted, as long as they adapted the right mind-set, not scared to work hard for it and then follow through taking action for what they truly wanted.

I realised, through all the articles I had done, it was another way of connecting with people that weren't on Instagram, as my audience of males and females could range from young teens all the way up to 60–80 years of age. So, I wanted to get together other platforms in order to reach other audiences, such as a website, Facebook, Twitter and a YouTube channel. I decided to start with the latter as everyone had been asking me if I had a channel yet, and so, I set to work on putting together my first video and working out content for my channel. This was a slower approach for me as filming and editing weren't my strongest points and took up more time than just posting a picture up on Instagram with a caption that came more naturally to me. So, I worked away at that slowly alongside my Instagram, again trying to share and spread my story further, developing content from what my followers wanted to know, based on their popular questions.

I was really spurred on by my social media platforms and had so much love for all the people that followed me. It's really like this wasn't about me anymore, but about them. I had to keep it up and keep going as I knew there were people I was encouraging to get healthy and fit from the messages I was receiving, and all their likes and comments were always so lovely and encouraging. It really made it all so worth it, not just for me, but knowing from my real account on weight loss, that anyone can do this, was helping someone else!

Chapter 30
Popular Weight-Loss Questions, Issues and Solutions

As I went about my everyday life, there were constantly new things for me to address and tackle in my new body and days as the 'healthy' new me. I'm glad I went through every one of these experiences, as it seems the things I was going through were also the most popular questions I was receiving on my Instagram account from my followers also on their own journeys. So, it was easy for me to relate, and in turn, answer these questions as best I could from my real-life account of each and every single question I was getting. I was like a walking-weight-loss-encyclopaedia! Nothing was off topic to me, and there was nothing I was shocked to hear and be asked, or didn't know how to go about answering.

So, I spent the remaining months of 2016, really embracing any hurdle, new experience, and weight loss problem, (which were not such a problem after all). Almost excited when I came face to face with any obstacle that I knew this would be a new experience and learn, to share with my followers. Tackling them head on, wanting to find the best and most efficient way of solving these issues and common queries in order to be able to feed back to the masses.

These seemed to be common problems for people all over the globe, and maybe not enough honest real or simple information out there by the sounds of things, as I kept getting the same question over and over.

So, here it goes, a whole chapter dedicated to a bunch of the popular questions I have received from you all throughout my journey and still to this day get weekly. Queries and questions that sometimes can even turn the most dedicated person off wanting to lose weight in the first place before they've even attempted to begin, or scare them off altogether before they've even given themselves a chance to just try! Thinking it's just too hard, or they don't want to face these issues, as they've heard how difficult they can be (also from someone who has never tried, just hear-say about weight loss myths). But fear not, my lovelies, you can and will overcome all of them! If I did, you can too.

Loose Skin

OK, OK, now, this must have been one of the most popular questions I got on my Instagram, which people were often really nervous to ask about. But if you know me by now, nothing is off limits or taboo, and I was always happy to talk about this topic, as in hindsight, it's something that can actually scare a lot of people off losing weight in the first place. That's the bit that used to upset me the most with this question.

I had been told by both people in real life and from my followers on Instagram that were obese, who had been thinking about losing weight for some time, that one of the reasons they had put it off for so long was that they were afraid to, because of the loose skin you are left with after a mass weight loss journey.

For this, we have to remember, yes, skin is an issue with weight loss, but I always try to think about what is worse for your health in the long run? Being overweight leading to many more health implications later in life like heart disease, diabetes, blood clots, thyroid problems or the loose skin? Excessive skin is not going to harm your health like fat will to your body and arteries.

I know it can have a confidence side effect instead, as we see these images of weight loss stories all over the magazines, and TV shows across the globe of these people standing there proud of their before and after weight loss pictures, holding layers and layers of lose skin drooping from their thinner bodies. Almost like they are now wearing an oversized deflated fat-suit. This is where I can relate, as I too once use to worry about the aftermath, and think to myself, 'what will I do with my lose skin? Will I have to get it removed, can I afford that, do I actually want to have an operation, if I have to? What about the scars?' So many questions all rolled in to one…what if, what if…but instead of worrying if you will have problems with skin, do something about it and I guess time will tell, you will find out soon enough!

The thing you have to constantly tell yourself is losing weight will do more for you overall than not losing it at altogether. Like I've said, I know I had people say to me that they thought the appearance of really loose skin was worse than them being overweight and the look of their size, so instead, they did nothing about it at all. So, it does have to come down to your own priorities and what is more important to you? I do feel, however, instead of worrying about one problem to avoid another, tackle one first, losing the weight, if that is what you really want long-term, and we can worry about combating the skin as we go through the journey and after it.

I can guarantee you one thing though, once you lose the weight, and yes, you may have some saggy skin, you are not going to regret that and wish you still had all the weight. No one ever lost 10, 20, 50 kg and then said to themselves 'I wish I didn't do that.' That is a fact. So, clear the stigmas from your mind of loose skin, because there are ways that can help and aid it to go back.

Each and everybody's skin is going to react differently because of certain factors from your life and your make up:

- How long have you been severely over weight and subsequently, the time the skin has been stretched for – The longer it is, yes, the more damaged the elastin can be, and this is just a point to be patient that the skin can take a little longer to rebuild that elastin.
- The age you are when you decide to start losing the weight for good – As we age, particularly during the years of 25–30, elastin and collagen production begins to slow down. These are two vital elements we need for skin cells recovery and rejuvenation to help shrink back down to your new bodies size after weight loss. So, yes, the older we are, the slower our skin may recover. However, this does not mean it won't!

- How quickly you lost the weight in the first place and what did you do to get there – Here is the one big benefit about losing weight like I did, the long-haul way. Skin can shrink and spring back, tightening over time, but it is an organ that responds at a much slower rate, than the time we actually took to lose the fat. This can sometimes take twice as long as it's taken your body to lose the actual weight. Hence why we see saggy skin. So, if you rush weight loss going on mad detoxes, having drastic surgery etc…the skin can be more obvious, as it hasn't had proper time to shrink back. But if you go about your weight loss over a realistic time period, it gives your skin cells time to start adjusting and rebuilding the cells, coming in like your body shape already has too.

- Nutrition, Health and Age – Your overall nutrients, what you are putting in your body, vitamins, mineral and water intake is crucial for skin to be getting as much as it needs to rebuild and constantly having cells re-growing. Foods rich in good fats, omega 3's, nuts, seeds, collagen rich green leafy vegetables, and foods rich in beta-carotene and Vitamin A (usually your red and orange fruit and veg) as all as foods with good quality protein can help repair damage. These are just a few routine things you should be aware of to be helping skin cells naturally. Your overall health, and hereditary factors can also affect your skins condition along with the age you are now. Don't we wish we could all have baby bottom skin for life!

- Smoking, Alcohol and Sun Damage – Avoid, avoid, avoid! Overexposure to the sun, especially sun damage and sun burn is really damaging the skins cells and their condition, doing the opposite of repair, so just be aware of this if you live in a hotter climate or use sun beds frequently. Along with smoking, which limits oxygen and reduces blood flow around the skin cells, leaving skin dry and dehydrated, neither of which is good for healthy nourished skin, alcohol has a similar effect which can also dry it out and deprive the skin of essential vitamins and nutrients it needs for growth.

As mentioned, skin can take a while to go back, so don't get impatient with it. Give it time and nurture it, it's the largest organ in our body and needs care, just like our hearts, lungs and brain throughout this weight loss journey—it's part of it too, you know—holding us together!

If, like me, you particularly suffer with the popular problem areas around the arms, inner thighs and lower stomach, it's probably cause these are also coincidentally our stubborn fat store areas in women (love handles, back fat and upper stomach for men), And often, the worst loose skin areas go side by side with our worst stubborn fat areas too. If there is still a lot of fat inside the skin pockets, the skin won't go back as tight, you need to really work on ridding the fat underneath, so the skin will snap back too. So, these were a few of the things I tried throughout my journey, don't wait till the end, work with your skin throughout the fat loss journey, as it's all part of your body transformation:

- Cardio and Weight Training – Both are great for burning fat, but weights are essential to get that muscle moving under the skin. As muscles are contracting, they are working the skin over that muscle and area, aiding in getting circulation to the cells and in fact, training the skin as well at the same time.

- Massage – Getting one from a professional is great, but what's stopping you from doing it yourself at home instead, pampering yourself and getting to know your body even better! It's highly beneficial as massage is great for bringing circulation and heat to the areas, both vital for skin growth, repair and rebuilding as well as increasing blood flow to the muscle and ligaments, which is great for the body in general. Massage creams containing Vitamin E or Coconut oil are great and should be rubbed in to the areas in circular motions for 5–10 minutes one to two times a day if you can. (Plus, your skin will feel great too—win win!)
- Sea Salt Scrubs – Exfoliating the whole body once a week will help remove old dead skin cells, as well as aiding in blood flow and circulation, rejuvenating the skin and making it healthier.
- Dry Body Brushing – This is basically as the name suggests, using a natural firm bristle brush, and brushing the skin usually from the feet upwards, or from the arms down, towards the heart or lymphatic nodes throughout the body. (There are many demonstrations on the internet, so have a search and see.) It is another form of increasing circulation and blood flow to the surface of your skin and exfoliating. It is also really great for helping the flow of our lymph system and getting rid of toxins in the body. So, a double-whammy with added benefits, so it's definitely worth one to add to the routine not just for help with skin.
- Limit sun exposure – Especially sun burn to the problem areas as this damages and kills the good cells that you already have in your skin and can make your skin appear more aged than it already is. If you are out and about enjoying the sun rays, make sure to use a good SPF sun cream and be aware of how long you are spending in the sun.
- Reduce (or quit) smoking – As mentioned above, besides, it being generally bad for your health, smoking and the chemicals contained in cigarette smoke are limiting oxygen to the cells, and doing the opposite of what you need for healthier skin cells. I know it's easier said than done quitting, I went through this too, but I really did feel better for it all over, and I can hear feel my lungs are loving me for it! (Especially when I attempt to run.)
- Vitamins and Minerals – Making sure we are getting enough good minerals and vitamins on the inside helps our skin on the outside, so make sure you are getting enough foods containing Vitamin A for that collagen and elastin production, E and C for fighting free radicals and helping with anti-ageing properties as well as foods rich in antioxidants, for healthier all-round skin.
- Rehydration – Ask yourself how much water you are drinking daily? Not including teas and coffees as they are actually dehydrators. You may not feel thirsty, but maybe your skin is? Two litres a day is the average recommended minimum for your body in a resting state, but if you are exercising and sweating on the daily, you really should be increasing your

water intake to three litres or more as our skin cells are made up of part water and rely on hydration just like we do to survive. Quench its thirst!

- So, there we are my top factors to be aware of and my top tips to combat all those skin woes! Like I said, never be afraid to lose weight because of what your skin may be like after, take care of your body now before it gets worse. Worrying doesn't solve anything, except wastes time. My skin is slowly going back over time as my weight was big for so long, it may not be perfect and still has saggy areas to it, but in time, I know it will get better and better, and I know that's from everything I've been doing throughout my journey to aid its recovery. There is a chance that one day, I may choose to get surgery to remove any excess skin, although I'd rather not, but I haven't ruled it out completely yet. But until then, I will keep doing everything I possible can for it. So, be patient and love the skin you're in.

Plateaus

The point where you have been working so hard, seeing great results week on week and then everything just stops! Kaput! Nada! No more results! I'm sure a lot of us can relate. Then you get irritated, fed up and just give up altogether right…wrong! That is not the solution. Most people see a plateau as a bad thing, but in hindsight, it's not really and in some ways, you should be proud of all the hard work you've been putting in—change your mentality here. A plateau can in a way mean it's all been working, and now your body has caught up to your mind games. It's advanced and become that healthier version to which all the hard work, exercise and healthy eating was for, right? So, why do we see it as a bad thing, that's what you wanted? A healthier fitter you, and the body has caught on and done what you wanted. You should be proud, congratulations, I say!

Never give up because you hit this plateau period, giving up ain't going to advance you any further and get you more results, right? If anything, it's going to send you 10 times backwards. Hovering around the same body weight fluctuating up and down a kilo or two is completely normal as well, and nothing to suddenly start panicking about.

Instead, acknowledge this plateau period where your body has levelled out and now, it's time to change it up again. Keep that body guessing again. In my initial two year transformation, I went through 3–4 big plateaus, and I took it all in my stride as a learning curve to then try something new to further myself and become even better, fitter and stronger in mind and body. Yep, that's right, a plateau is a chance to level up!

Each time I experienced this point where my results started to slow down, I acknowledged, and felt proud for everything that I had been doing, and although I may not have seen drastic results on the outside as much, I remembered still what all of this was doing for my insides and overall well-being. I took the opportunity to then change up my routine, and here are a few of the things I tried during my own plateaus:

Try new exercises to add to the weight training for each body part.
- Experiment with variations of sets and reps.

- Changing the weight increments you're doing at the time, adding more variety; having a light week, other times having a very heavy week.
- Introduce new types of cardio as well as the intensity and duration, including HIIT and LISS.
- Try out new sports all together, away from the gym.
- Change the time of day you're exercising.
- Introduce new foods, swapping out items for even healthier items now your taste buds are getting used to them; it's a chance to get even healthier than you have already become!
- Try eating variations of food groups. For instance, if you always have chicken, try turkey or Salmon or vice versa.
- Alter the veg and fruit you have constantly, experiment with new ones.
- Change the time of day you are eating, if you can.
- Remember, as you are getting healthier, slimmer or leaner, that you are eating for your current body type and the right amount of calories, not eating for the body you were 6–12 months earlier (depending on how far in to your journey you are).

Now, you don't have to change everything at once, pick a few things you can implement to alter your current food and exercise routine, save some other things to try on the next plateau because if you are on a long journey like I was, you may face another, but now, you know what is happening with your body and how to tackle it.

Always remember change is a good thing, it means your body has got comfortable again, it's all working, and now it's time to push on forward to the next stage of your journey!

Calorie Counting

Yes, the bit we all either love or hate, 100 here, 300 there, micros, macros…what? OK, let's get down to basics with this one. It's completely up to you how you count your food and what works for you in a positive way, not a mental chore that suddenly takes over your entire life and you've got your calculator and note pad out all day long.

You can't let this control you, but I do feel it is incredibly important to know what you are putting in your body versus what you are out putting in activity. If not, how do you know your surplus, and what is right for you in terms of calories and what you want to burn if, indeed, you are wanting to lose weight?

Throughout my entire journey, I never did the whole counting macros thing, I just decided that wasn't for me, each to their own, I know some people swear by it. I did, however, count calories to a rough estimate. Especially as this has always been my biggest problem, as you know I could hoover down 4,000 calories in an hour. So, for me, this was something I decided to do, especially in the early days on my journey, getting myself down from my 4,000–5,000 average calorie day to the 2,000 range, the national recommended amount for women. Now, this is a guide given across the world, and we are all different, but I feel it's a good place to start.

It will also help you to figure out your BMR, your basal metabolic rate, which is a rough estimate of how many calories you'd burn if you were to do nothing but sit still for 24 hours. It gives us an indication of the minimum amount of energy needed to keep your body functioning, e.g. breathing, your heart beating, organs functioning.

There are lots of calculators available on the internet to do this for you or most gyms or pharmacies have a machine you can do this on as well.

When I first did mine from memory, it was around 1,800 calories that I needed based on my height, age, weight, muscle mass, water weight etc…so then I had to figure out on average how many calories I was burning per day in exercise and add it to my BMR, and let's say for the purpose of this it 700 calories a day I was burning, I would add that on and my total was 2,500 all up I could have ate to fuel my body's resting rate plus the exercise I was doing. But since I was trying to lose weight, I then knew I could eat roughly 2,000 or so calories a day and still be burring off fat as I was in a surplus of -500.

This is simple way of figuring it and how your body can operate, now I'm no scientist or sports nutritionist, but if you want to lose weight it goes without saying you have to burn more than you consume. But you do not need to under eat and starve yourself.

You do, however, need to be conscious of what is in the calories you are eating each day as well, enough good fats, carbs, fibre, protein etc…and yes, that is where people then start to do their micros and macros, which I never did, I, instead, chose to be more self-aware of the foods I was eating, doing a lot of research and educating myself on food, limiting processed sugars, white carbs, processed foods and saturated fats. I always ate a high amount of veg and fruits, nuts, seeds and proteins as well as low GI carbs.

This is personally just how I decided to do my foods each day, I didn't want to get too bogged down and go in to a mental battle where I am living my life from a calculation of calories, so instead, I did rough figures and numbers in my head each day and still do. I'm now pretty good at knowing what calories are in everything I put in my mouth, that it's almost automatic in my head tallying up my daily threshold of calories versus how much time I'm being active.

Figure out a system that works for you, whether it's a food diary, an app on your phone, a full macro guide, whatever it is, do a system that works for you and you can maintain to help you, not beat you down.

Celebrations and Holidays

This is a topic a lot of people asked me more about in secret through direct messages. I received a lot of private questions about people who were not looking forward to an upcoming night out with the girls or a family holiday that was approaching, instead of being happy and looking forward to it.

Mainly, it came down to confidence in themselves and their goals, support from the people they were going to be around and lack of pride in the life they'd chosen from fear of begin judged.

Let's break that all down; for instance, one girl was almost going to turn down a big girly night out were they were going for take away and drinks because she knew the other girls were slimmer and had never worried about weight in her eyes, and that they would sit there with an almost lack of understanding of how she felt, and encourage her to just eat and drink, saying 'who cares' or 'it's just one night, live a little'. I felt for her because I too had been through something similar with friends who didn't quite understand how important my journey was to me in the start. But I always stood my ground, that bit is important, we are all different, some people can eat and look like they'll never gain a pound, other people like me, I can just look at chocolate and gain 10! So, we all have our boundaries and limitations.

If you know a holiday or big night out is coming up, think about what you really want to do, and that does not include not going (yes, I hear some of you saying this to me!) You need to decide for that period of time you are away or out for the night, is it a celebration where you want to indulge and you deserve it and have it as your reward or cheat day, or why not have healthier options on the menu too?

There are always options, you still can go out and enjoy yourself, and it does help to surround yourself with good family and friends who know how important this lifestyle is to you.

I know sometimes with family dinners or in-laws in particular, that you don't want to be rude so you feel you have to eat the food. But it's not rude, why do we have to eat everything. For instance, you wouldn't force someone of a Muslim religious background to eat pork, or a vegan to eat fish, so if you choose a certain lifestyle and food group then stand by it, unless, of course, you want to have a treat and feel you can that day. It doesn't matter what the old you used to eat and drink, this is the new you and your taste buds have changed! Period!

What I also tend to do, especially with upcoming holidays, is make sure the run up to such events or celebrations I am extra good, so the vacation or party is like a little reward in my journey to have a break, let my hair down in moderation, but still integrate my life, similarly to what I did on my vacations during my weightless journey. I embrace both the holiday and the lifestyle I now live!

I chose holidays where there is a great health club or gym nearby, or outdoor exercise facilities like pools or the beach, or simply walking around the new city instead of getting public transport. Then on return, or the day after a big night out, I always make sure I am right back in to my routine right away.

We should be able to have the balance in our lives, where we are not fearing events, but can enjoy them and be happy with the life we have chosen. Stop worrying what other lives people have chosen for themselves, and often, if someone says, "Oh, come on, Carli just have one tiny bit," or "It's only one shot," and I say "No, thanks, why don't you have it instead." Their response is usually a no too…funny that. Don't give in to peer pressure because that is what the old you would have done, and your friend isn't used to the new you, so show them who you are now.

Ask yourself, do you actually want it? Do you need it? Or will you feel guilty? Go with your gut instinct and mindful reasoning, it's much better than letting someone else think for you, unless they are great friends encouraging you to be healthy and stick to your hard work! Yes, listen to those lovely people too!

Each holiday and event will differ, but do what is right for you, your body and lifestyle, enjoy yourself in moderation, but be conscious of how you will feel the morning after and use that as a guide for your decision making.

Fads and Diets

Okay, so by now you will know I am totally against all this gimmick stuff, and I can proudly speaking from experience that they really aren't worth it. I think I literally have tried some of the weirdest things on the market.

Back when I was younger, I'd often try anything I saw on TV or in a magazine advert that some celeb was endorsing, partly because it looked cool, or said it worked miracles (said being the operative word, no proven results mind you...)

I did meal replacement shakes, about four different brands, I did fat burner pills, again trying any new ones that came to market, I tried waist trainers, and sweat suits—yes, like a Michelin man, I tried wraps, and I even tried a little magical seed in water before bed at night (LOL!) Yes, all because marketing campaigns said they were the new thing to make you lose weight.

But NO, no they weren't. You may see tiny results for 1, 2, 3 weeks, but these are not sustainable for life! Here is my point here. Diets to me mean failure. An end date taking you 10 steps back, wasted time and money.

Crash diets, juicing and detoxes where you are on very low calories for a number of weeks and see the scales dropping is often the result of you actually losing water and glycogen stows in your body. It's not sustainable long-term or for life, so the moment you eat real food regularly again, it will all come back. There is no shortcut for good health with these things.

Say, you try a detox for one month and spend all this, obey it, then next month, you try a waist trainer, month three on to meal replacement shakes, month four, you're trying some minus 1,000 calorie diet, month five you're doing wraps and month six, now on to fat burners...that's six months of time, maybe with few pounds gone here and there, but are you going to keep all these fads up for 20–30 years? And how about the £500 + money you've spent buying all these things?

When there are people who tell me eating healthy is expensive, but will happily spend 100s on fads. What about if you took that £500 and the six months, and really invested it in YOU? Taking small steps each day to exercise, eat better, buy your own foods to cook, maybe bought a few pieces of gym equipment off eBay, or a budget gym membership, you'd probably still have £100 left over to buy yourself a nice dress at the end of the six months and be 1–2 dress sizes down, with weight that will stay off, a healthier inside and a new mind-set to actually keep at it. To me, that's a six months well spent and satisfaction at the end of it, instead of a wasted six months, and disappointment from the fads with no results and £500 down the drain.

Think about it, time is going to pass anyway, and I can only speak from experience, but hey, when I stopped looking at all these fads, that if they were really wonderful and amazing, there would be one the entire world was doing and everyone would be super slim, and instead, looked at myself, and thought right, it may seem like the long haul, hard work way, but you know what it really is the only way long-term that is going to work and make me healthy all over.

Even weight loss surgery, which I understand for some people is a last resort, but if by any chance you can do it without surgery, I would recommend it. It gives a change for your body's organs to recover, your skin to go back, your mind-set to change and for you to spend time getting to know yourself.

Trust me, if you take one bit of advice from this, please invest your interest, money, energy and time in yourself. It is so worth it!

Supplements

Throughout my journey, alongside my healthy eating, I have used some supplements, more so in the first 1–2 years of my journey than I do now. I've never been against supplements, I just don't feel I need them, or actually want them in my daily diet anymore as much.

With any kind of supplement, please, please, please ask yourself what are you taking it for?

I hear so many people saying they are taking this protein powder and this energy enhancer etc, etc, and I ask them, do they actually know what's in it or why they are taking it and at what point in the day is best? And 9 times out of 10, they have no answer for any of these questions.

Half the people tell me they are taking protein powder cause they see all the girls standing there with the shakers in their hands posing in Instagram pics and they think it helps to lose weight because these girls look super slim and shredded…insert face-palm emoji here…that is incorrect.

If you want to take things to add to your daily diet, do some research and find out: A) What are the products for? B) What is in the products in terms or ingredients and additives? C) What are the benefits? And lastly, but most importantly, D) Do you need to add this or can you get it from food, vitamins, minerals before reaching for a supplement?

I found some people were taking 300–400 calories of protein powder a day in between meals, but not really accounting for those calories…it all adds up and has to go somewhere. You could have 4–5 eggs instead and actually fill you up, or a large chicken breast.

My point is, don't just jump on the band-wagon of having supplements because you see people down the gym or on social media doing it—again sometimes another marketing ploy to sell you rubbish. But if you find there are things that are worth-to adding to your daily intakes then yes, do it.

With protein powders, there are a variety of ones to choose from made from a main base of either whey, beef, casein, soya and pea or other plant based proteins, which are all a personal preference. I don't mind a good quality protein powder, if I'm on the go, or can't make a good meal right after the gym and have a longer drive home or something similar (but in all honestly, this is probably only once a month if that, it's there as a last resort for me, and I think the tub in my cupboard has probably gone off by now LOL!) I do like to cook with protein powders on occasion, mostly using vegan or pea protein powders these days, in replace of flours in cakes, pancakes, protein balls or even bean burgers and falafel mixes.

Pre-workout powders and drinks are another thing that I feel a lot of the young lads like to take to look cool at how many scoops they can take without water to show how hard they are in the gym, before even lifting a dumbbell…again face-palm emoji insert here…

Pre-workouts can be a good workout booster, but again, check the ingredients, some can be quite strong and give you a tingling effect all over you may not be prepared for, or enjoy the feeling of either. Your body can also become dependent on these and eventually immune, doing nothing for you. It's maybe once or twice a year now I would have one if I felt I really needed it through a massive heavy session, but I feel I rely on natural energy to get me through a workout and pure determination, or if all else fails a bloody good strong coffee is my secret weapon of choice, I'll take that any day and a good night sleep in advance over a pre-workout!

Protein bars are selling like hot cakes these days, and pretty much a 'healthier version' of a chocolate bar filled with protein but still with fake sugars. These are ones you really should read the labels and check the ingredient quantities as I'm sure half the ingredients in some of the really processed bars you probably can't even pronounce or know what it is. So, instead I'm all for making these myself and take one with you to the gym to have after if you feel you need it. You can then enjoy them knowing they are actually healthy, and doing something good for you and your muscles in that recovery and repair stage after a good workout. There are plenty of recipes online to choose from and much better for you, so be careful downing too many of these thinking they are doing something great for your body, you're better off going home and having a good protein packed meal and maybe a small treat after.

The list of supplements and jars of powders, pills and bars goes on, but one I don't mind too much is BCAAs AKA Branch Chain Amino Acids. This is one of the only supplements I find really does help with rebuilding and growth in the body and putting back in what we may not get enough of from food. Essentially, they are 20 amino acids that are the building blocks that make up protein, which either we get from food or our bodies try to produce enough of for growth and rebuilding. With these, I will try choose one you get a good mix of all amino acids with as little additives and flavourings as possible, and I have it occasionally in my water throughout the day. Again, I'm not religious with having this every day, but if I was to choose just one supplement to have, it would be BCAAs as the rest I feel I can get enough from foods.

My point with sups is to just do your research, there are thousands of pages on the internet of people giving their opinions, reviews, studies etc…find what works for you, but like I said, know why you are taking it, not because your gym buddy does or the insta-model you follow does, who probably doesn't even use the product herself, she just gets paid to post it! Be smart, it's your body, not theirs!

Cheat and Rest days

Throughout my journey, I've never been a planner of when my cheat day or my rest day will be. My only rule is they are not on the same day.

When I first started, cheat days were obviously days I looked forward to as this was all new to me and conditioning out of eating all the crap food I used to eat I still enjoyed this day, very much so! But you have to learn to do it right, a cheat day or cheat meal rather, does not mean you have to or should eat every bad item in sight. It's more a reward at the end of a great week or consecutive days, when you can have a meal you've bee craving. I usually do it after my biggest session of the week, which was usually legs, so my metabolism was high and still in calorie burning mode after my workout. But I really went on that gut feeling with this, sometimes, I may have had a cheat meal every 5–6 days, or sometimes go 10 days, or even on the odd occasion, I had two mini cheats in the week, like maybe it was someone's birthday in the office and I had cake, then opted for a burger and salad on the weekend.

You have to be sensible here, and know yourself well, if I went too long without, I feared I may cave and binge, but I also didn't want to have them too frequently that I started to get the taste back for sugars and fats that once ruled my life.

One thing I did notice though, was over time, my cheat meals weren't really such a cheat anymore, majority of the time. As my taste buds got healthier and healthier alongside my love of eating well, my 'cheat' meals turned out to be just nice dishes, or elaborate flavoursome good food I maybe didn't eat as often—even going to for a steak, sweet potato fries and a light dessert was something out of the ordinary to me now, or rather just not an everyday meal for me, so having it every week or so, felt like a treat to my taste buds and brain. Now, this meal is not incredibly bad for me, just out of the norm of my usual daily eating routine, was enough to make me feel like I'd had something different and satisfying.

I actually can' t remember the last time I had takeaway, as I make all my own Mexican, Indian or Asian style food myself from scratch, I haven't had a pizza in about six months or McDonalds in over two years (and I honestly never miss it). I love to make homemade healthy burgers and even eat majority of vegan cakes and treats now too—so in essence, my not so healthy foods—are actually not so bad for me in reality. But if I was to go all out, a big cheat meal to me would probably be more so indulging in a few extra calories, as you all know, I love my calories! LOL! For me, a cheat is having a main, a side and a dessert—a full blown meal— could be a so-so healthy meal, but it's just having more that I usually would.

With your cheat, choose something you've been craving, enjoy it, eat it slowly, savour it! Sit down and eat it properly and know you earned it. Don't feel guilty about it either! Then once it's gone, it's gone, OK! Know there is always next week, you don't need more now.

For rest days, I also don't schedule these either, surprise, surprise! I listen to my body. I've gone 31 days before with no rest, and I've also had weeks with two rest days back to back. We are all different so I go on how I feel each day.

Some rest days to me still involve a swim, walk or yoga class, other rest days are literally a complete rest, sitting on the couch, Netflix and chill kinda day. I often do struggle to do nothing, but yes, yes, I know it's good for my body and recovery, so I do it. Often, I can feel worse off throughout the day if I don't exercise in the morning, feeling more sluggish and lethargic, as I'm used to morning exercise really getting me going and waking me up so to speak. But I just make sure to eat well that day, have plenty of water, and foods full of nutrients and keep my calories around my recommendation from the BMR calculation, and of course, get plenty of sleep! A day of rest and relaxation never hurt anybody!

Weigh Days

Yes, the day we either love or loathe, battling our love or hate relationship with those bathroom scales! This can come down to personal preference and how it effects everyone can be different. My advice though is take control over whatever you decide to do! Some people weigh themselves every day, some to once a week, some once a fortnight, and some not at all.

I do feel you need to have some form or measuring and tracking throughout your journey, if not, how are you going to track your progress? Some people decide to take body measurements instead, which is great too, and could be worth doing both, although, if you don't get the same circumference on your body each week, your results may not be accurate.

I did choose to weigh myself pretty much every day during the start of my journey as I almost enjoyed it, starting my day that way every morning, then slowly, I dropped it down to every second or third day.

There was a period I stopped weighing myself altogether and I feel like I went backwards a little bit, not keeping track properly, so I then went to once a week, and felt that is now right for me.

Although I'm not obsessive about it, I don't get down or irritated if I go up a kilo here and there. Weight fluctuations are natural and we all have them, so don't beat yourself up. It's actually more often than not to do with water retention or bloating and even the salt in our body, so even more of a reason to reduce unwanted salts, eat healthy, and drink plenty of water, because contrary to fact, water actually helps flush out water, the salt causing water retention!

So, find a system and regular 'check-in' day that works for you, where it isn't going to affect your mentality with weight loss but more be a guide to keeping you on track and motivated.

****

I hope these have answered some of your questions, if not already answered throughout my book, but since these were the ones that were the most popular on my Instagram and deserved a longer answer than the captions allow on social media, I'm hoping this has given you an insight in to what I've found worked for me to best answer these for you all, and hope that you can use them too if you face such situations on your own health and fitness paths.

Chapter 31
Opinions

One thing that I did really notice post weight loss as I was getting smaller, is how I was treated compared to when I was overweight, being that it was slightly different to when I was big. Now, I don't think I experienced this on the same scale I've seen or heard other people go through, but it made me aware this really does happen.

When I was larger, I think being confident and happy in my own skin really did help, as I wore my size with pride and owned it, so maybe I didn't receive as many nasty or bullying comments to my face, but I'm sure I did behind my back. Similar to that mother and daughter in the South of France that time.

As I lost the weight and became slimmer, I did notice more attention from not only the opposite sex in terms of dating and having more guys approach me than at my previous size, but even with old friends, or acquaintances that maybe weren't as friendly or warm and welcoming as to when I was obese, were suddenly wanting to be best buds and know what I was up to with my life.

Although the oddest thing was from strangers, as when I was larger, I would get stared at, or people watched me when I ate, just as I had once down to that boy in Mexico, or the odd bullying comments walking past me on the street about my size. For instance, on a work get-away to Barcelona in the very early days of my weight loss journey, I remember riding a Segway around the town sightseeing, and a guy actually yelled out at me that I was lazy and should be walking not riding a Segway because of my size. But little did he know, I was already about 30 kg down in my journey and had actually probably walked for five hours that day and this was something we wanted to do that afternoon. See, you never know what journey someone is already on, and to be honest, what business was it of his, so, of course, I laughed my loudest laugh at him, grinned and waved in true Carli style, as I rode my Segway directly at him! Come on, I just had to LOL!

But the way he yelled out at me, anyone would have thought he had the right to be treating me like I was a criminal or doing something bad in the streets of Barcelona, just because of my size. Being overweight does not make people horrible, but there is this odd hate in society for fat people. I've never truly understood it, but it's like a disapproving kind of hate in a way, more so from people that have never even been over weight a day in their lives and can't comprehend how people get so big in the first place. We are not rapists, or murderers, we are just fatter people. Yes, I get it, but trust me there are worse things in the world to hate or disapprove of people for, rather than the size they are, we all have hearts on the inside.

But I guess this opened up my eyes to the way mentalities and opinions of others are instilled in your ways of thinking and perceptions, also from a young age growing up and parents sharing their views with you. Not comparing the two entirely, but it's a slightly similar stereotyping that people do with cultures, races, sexualities, disabilities etc...people decided they do or don't like you based on a characteristic, trait, belief or way of life. Now, this is all a much deeper topic, but I just found it interesting as to how people can treat people because they are overweight.

To an extreme, I know a lot of people can be severely bullied and even in the current social media world we live in, be trolled online by people for begin fat. I was lucky in a way, I only had the 1–2 odd comments on my Instagram compared to some receiving repetitive bullying on their pages, but even with these few comments I got, it actually didn't bother me, with my amazing followers being quick to defend me and retaliate at them, I chose not to, instead I asked these lovely followers to not waste their good energy attacking, but instead, I acknowledged the bullying person and showed them love. I wasn't going to stoop to their level or antagonise them like they probably wanted me to do, instead I just said I appreciate they had their opinion and views, but not everyone is the same in this world, and if they can't accept that, then maybe they need to focus their energy on themselves instead of me and love themselves just a little bit more. But I appreciated them coming to visit my page every day, and loved how concerned they were about me and my story—it was touching really! LOL! They went away shortly after that...

I guess I've always had this way with negativity or nasty comments and people, they just don't really seem to faze me in the slightest, especially from people I don't know in life. Their opinion really means so little to me, it's not worth me getting worried about. I'm happy with who I am and the life I chose to live, and the life I live now. If anything, I feel sorry for those people with such narrow minds and opinions, they could do with just being a bit more open and less judgemental, being happier and not worrying about what others are doing and just living their own best life.

In life, we will always come up against people that are brought up in different ways, believe their own myths and perceptions, and that's life I guess, we will never all think the same. Accepting that is part of it.

But I even got it from friends or acquaintances, such as one male friend who was a body builder and had literally never had an ounce of fat on him in his entire life. He once said to me, that he didn't get it how people got so big in the first place, he didn't understand how people couldn't just stop eating. I really did try to explain that life-long obesity and the mental implications are very different to a guy having a little beer belly for a year or so, or a life-long slim woman trying to lose some post pregnancy weight, both equally challenging, but severe obesity comes with a lot of extra things to consider when wanting to lose weight for good. Although I don't think he really got my point when he said, "Why don't you just lock yourself away in a room and eat peanuts for a month or so..." and I realised then that some people will just never get it or understand obesity, because the worst bit was he was serious about his suggestion. (Face palm emoji yet again!)

If it was so easy, the entire world would be so slim and slender and we would have no overweight people, or issues with fat and obesity right!

But one bit I did think helped me throughout all my varying sizes was just owning it, and taking control of the things I could change, and not worrying about society and others' views of the morbidly obese. There will always be someone that dislikes you 'cause you're fat, that's a fact, but you know what I'm sure not everyone likes them for their personality, that's also a fact! So live and let live in the best way you can for yourself and don't lose sleep over the opinions of others! Just love yourself and do what you can to be your best!

Chapter 32
One Step Closer to Where
I Want to Be

So, as we begin a new year, 2017 started off with a bang literally! Like everything I had been imagining, visualising in that brain of mine and working for in real life, was coming together slowly. I could just feel it.

Looking back at this year just gone, it really has been immense for me, not so much in just weight loss goals and the physical look of my body goals, but more so everything I've been working for over the last three years is coming together. My whole life has really transformed, edging towards making a career from what I've achieved with my body goals and using all the hard work to make something of myself.

That's the thing with any big goal, aspirations, dreams and plans, you can't rush it. A lot of people in our generation want it now, now, now! With the popularity on social media and reality TV growing, people see a certain image portrayed and think it looks super easy, so people want, want, want! But maybe don't necessarily see the hard work that really goes alongside all the good things, and aren't prepared to work, work, work for it!

Often the behind the scenes effort people are putting in is not shown as much, AKA, the grind is sold separately! And just the aftermath and glamorous side is shown through the wonderful world of social media.

You really have to go about it all the right way, keeping at it every day, never giving up, staying in your lane, focusing forward on what you want, and not worrying about what others are doing! Then and only then, you'll find you get closer every day! Use your energy wisely and on what matters to you most.

Without realising it, 9 times out of 10, you are exactly where you are meant to be, everything is happening around you, sometimes without even knowing it as sometimes, we forget to just live in the moment as well. So, keep at it, working away on those plans and dreams. You may not quite see what you're working for just yet, but oh, trust me, and trust in the universe, everything you are doing is gearing you up and leading you to a moment yet to come. Just believe that, and keep working for everything you want, and putting your energy and effort in to the right places now!

With all that in mind, I really decided to take charge this year, and started off the year of 2017 really clearing out what no longer served me. What I mean by that is after almost a three year journey of self discovering and transforming my mind, body and life, I felt I had so much energy, help and love to give, and I was trying to help everyone around me as well still, but sometimes giving that energy to the wrong people or scenarios in life! I could only be at my best if I really channelled my energy on things where my energy and time was better spent. You know on the right things only!

So, I began clearing out anything, possession, person, situation, in my life that really didn't need, or yes, deserve me and my time…that energy was better spent elsewhere. I had chapters to close, so to speak, loose ends to tie up, emotionally and physically to really be able to move onwards and upwards with myself, as my best self, in the best state possible.

There was one chapter and part of my life in particular that had been playing on my mind recently, and most importantly, one thing I knew which was well over due to address…a much needed trip home to Sydney. Something I guess you could say I had been sort of (very much so) putting off re-visiting for years now, since 2012 actually.

I don't know why but it was like I loved my life here in the UK so much, and especially who I had become here. I had changed so much, yet felt more like me than I'd ever felt in my lifetime! Surrey and London would always have a special place in my heart, I'd lost half my body weight here, but gained so much more than I ever felt possible!

It was liking going back to Sydney would bring back so many memories both good and bad that I had overcome, either suppressed or surpassed, maybe both…emotions, childhood memories, big-Carli-days and all this stuff I had metaphorically shed, along with the actual weight itself, and this all felt so good now. I hadn't been back there since with my ex, almost five years ago now, and it was almost three years since I had since my mum, waving a teary goodbye at the airport in America all those years ago.

So much had changed in my life for the better, and I guess, symbolically, going back to Sydney felt like I was going backwards in my life, back to my old ways, the old me, things I had got rid of for good, like the bad habits, the bad lifestyle, and yes, ultimately the weight…I had been morbidly obese the entire time I'd lived in Australia. I felt like no one really knew me there anymore; I literally was a 360 in mind, body and soul of the old crazy partying-ways-Carli. I was almost a stranger to majority of the people I once knew back in Oz…not just by looks, but by personality too.

But I knew in my heart I had to go. I did really want to see my mum, catch up with some of my old friends, walk along Manly Beach with the sand between my toes, and see the sights I knew so well… *Geez*, I thought, *no one is going to recognise me!* Of course, my friends had seen pictures of the new me on Facebook and Instagram, but I guess in person, it's so different.

For my mum, being so old-fashioned, she didn't even have a smart phone; we had never facetimed or skyped in the seven years since I left Australia. No picture messages at all either! We were so old school when it came to our communication, we literally called or sent traditional SMS messages—LOL—I know right! All I could imagine was her face when she saw me, damn was she going to be in for one hell of a shock!

She too had only seen the magazine articles that went out in Australia, along with a few printed photos I had posted her in the mail, along with The Sun article from here in the UK, as well as being shown my Instagram once or twice by people. *This is going to be monumental!* I thought.

So, with that all in mind and before I had time to change my mind, I searched flights to Sydney, Australia for March 2017, booked them right away, paid and that was it! Done!

I was going back to Sydney, my previous home, my home away from home really! I printed my boarding pass and posted it to my mum as a surprise! *Here we come, Sydney*, I thought, and nostalgia took over, I could smell the scent of Sydney already.

Chapter 33
Homewood Bound:
Sydney, Australia

I was really anxious the weeks leading up to the flight, I knew it was going to be an emotional journey in more ways than one, and I was going over and over so many memories and scenarios in my head.

As the week came to depart, it was actually the three year mark since I started my body transformation, it wasn't intentionally planned like that, but symbolic in a way really!

As I boarded my flight at Gatwick Airport, I was a mix of emotions. A usual lover of flying and especially on long haul flights, I thought this one was going to feel like an eternity, all alone with just my thoughts and feelings for 23 hours straight!

Surprisingly though, and to my relief, the journey actually felt really quick, and on the final leg of the trip after refuelling in Bangkok, I now just couldn't wait to get there. With my emotions all over the place, I was anxious, excited, nervous all at the same time, and as the wheels of the Boeing 747 came down to land on the familiar tarmac at Kingsford Smith Airport, I looked out the window, seeing all the tails of the Qantas jets, with their slogan Spirit of Australia and for some reason that always brings a wave of nostalgia over me.

I had made it, I was home. I had tears in my eyes, I don't know why, I was just so emotional. This had been a long time coming, a full 360 on my life, so much had happened since I had left, it had been years since I'd been back, and I didn't really know what the next three weeks here would hold for me or how I would feel. But I guess there was only one way to find out!

I disembarked the plane with the herds of people heading for immigration and out to the baggage hall. It was still so surreal I was here, almost seven years in total since I first left back in 2010 to embark on that big travelling trip of a lifetime. I took a minute by myself in the rest rooms to freshen up (pull myself together more like) and be proud of everything I had achieved in those seven years. *Wow* is literally what I thought, staring myself right in the eyes as I looked at myself in the mirrors.

I had left this very airport with no idea where my life would be heading to travel the world and find myself. And I really had done just that. So, with a big smile on my face, I felt like this was the round trip, I'd almost come back to close a door on one chapter of my life, so I could really move forward in to the new life I and been creating. I decided that's what this trip was going to be for me. A trip down memory lane, to acknowledge everything in my life, the good and the bad, that had made me what I'd become today. I didn't have to go backwards being here, instead I could be thankful for who I was now, and keep moving forward!

As my bags finally came round the carousel (I swear they are always the last), I hurled them off the conveyer belt and on to my trolley, quickly heading for the arrivals hall with anticipation. *Here we go!* I thought. I got my phone out and switched it to video. I just had to film my mum's reaction; her face is always priceless.

As I came through the doors to all the eagerly awaiting faces holding up name boards and eyes darting for their arrivals, I saw her familiar-mumsy face, hands waving about in the air, as mothers do.

I could already see she was welling up, mouth dropping at the same time, she was overwhelmed, shocked, excited and teary all at once seeing me half the size, but in general, you could see she was just excited to be seeing me after all this time! As we reached each other, we just hugged, her arms could actually fit around me this time, we were both crying, happy tears. In our blubbering messes, we could barely get our words out, repeatedly exchanging hugs and kisses, she just looked so happy to see me, like finally, I'd come back. (I'm welling up now just typing this remembering the feelings of the emotions that morning arriving in Sydney.)

I remember a girl next us was so touched by our emotional reunion, she too looked like she wanted to cry and actually offered to take a picture for us. So, you know me, never one to miss marking an occasion with a photo opportunity, I happily took her up on her offer, and I can still see the images now in my mind of us standing there tears and all.

It really was great to see her in person, not just exchanging text message and quick phone calls like we had done over the years, which had become so normal to us, but probably odd to so many other mother and daughters out there.

It felt just like old times, as if I'd never even gone, walking along the airport, we grabbed a couple of coffees before heading for the car. As we headed out the airport and the sliding doors opened, the smell of Sydney filled my nostrils, (it really did have this certain aroma to it and smells have such funny way of bringing back so many memories) I felt like I was 20 again. I knew this would be the first of many remembrances this trip so I better get used to it! I think the theme literally was going to be nostalgia the entire time I was here.

We drove the familiar route home over the Sydney Harbour Bridge, through the streets I knew so well of Mosman, near where I'd gone to school for so many years, over the Spit Bridge where I'd done rowing as a teen, and round the scenic streets of Fairlight all the way down to Manly Beach. As I saw the horizon and blue ocean for miles as we descended down the hill, it did feel good to be back, and I could smell the mix of salty air, sand and sea! Still, to this day, one of my favourite smells ever!

The first few days were like that, still a little overwhelmed, jet lagged and excited, I tried to settle in to a routine of normality. And the first thing on my mind was, where was the nearest gym? LOL! Yes, I missed it already after being stuck on a plane sitting done for nearly 24 hours!

But with the Manly Beach front at my door step, I utilised being in Oz during the warmer summer months and made the most of the outdoors, walking and jogging along the beach, as well as diving head first in to the beautiful ocean for a swim almost every day! That is one thing I had definitely missed being in the UK. I had always lived one minute from a beach, that was the norm to me growing up, and I don't think I really appreciated it or made the most of it when I did live in Australia, almost taking it for granted. Sometimes, it takes you to lose something, to realise how much you loved it and should have made more of it whilst you had it.

I also got a pass to the local Fitness First my mum was a member of, and for the first time ever in our lives, Mum and I got a proper gym session in together! Whoever would have thought!

I think it was about 3 days in to my trip, jet-lag well and truly had slapping me for 6, that the realisation and reality that I was back here in Sydney was kicking in, and even though I was in a place I had known so well, I was also feeling like a foreigner, on my own. I did have a little wobble and maybe even a slight panic attack. For a girl who had never ever felt homesick in her life, this was my first experience of that, missing my home in Surrey, being away from all my home comforts and true identity.

I had to be on my own for a bit that morning, collect my thoughts, and at one point even called a friend, needing to hear a familiar voice, saying how I wanted to get back on a plane to Heathrow real quick. I don't know what came over me, I felt like a stranger, in a place I had lived for over 24 years...

But after a few deep breaths, a walk by myself on the beach, I pulled myself together and snapped out of it. I realised that was a natural feeling after all this time, returning here by myself, worlds away from who I used to be. I talked some sense in to myself, that I needed to make the most of this trip as a holiday for me and embrace everything from Australia and that everything in my old life had got me to my new life! Tomorrow was a new day, I would start the trip a-fresh, with a good outlook to enjoy it all!

As the first week got underway, I didn't want to waste any more time, even though it felt like I had almost three weeks in Sydney, I knew it would eventually fly by, and I had so much I wanted to do, people to see and catch up with, and also relax a bit—I needed this as a vacation too!

I had a few different groups of friends from Sydney from different periods of my life, and it was great to see them all! Friends that were like family to me, who were now settling down having babies of their own, it was so beautiful to see, and glad that after all the years, miles apart and people growing in different directions that we can still remain friends to this day. I can't help but say that's one of my main loves of social media for people who live long distances apart, it feels like I see them every week sometimes and keeps us in touch with one another, but was great to see them in the flesh after all the years apart.

We chatted, gossiping and hearing all about each other's lives now! People's reactions to me and how I'd changed physically was lovely and made all the hard work I'd done really worth it. They didn't just see the change I had made in looks but me as a person, how much I'd grown and what I was doing with my life. I knew my true friends were really happy for me, and even though I had made the decision to leave Australia for good and the UK was now home, they knew I'd made the right decision for me.

Seeing all my girls from high school was amazing, and that is one set of people no matter where we end up in life we can always catch up as if we saw each other yesterday, and for this, I will always be forever grateful. In turn, I was so happy for all of them as well and proud of the lives they had all made for themselves, majority engaged, married, babies running about or on the way. I felt like we were all 18 again heading to our school formal, but no, we were all now grown women with lives and paths of our own. It's funny where life takes you hey!

I had a fantastic time catching up with everyone, spending some quality time with my mum, shopping at Westfield Warringah Mall, our local shopping centre, getting the famous Manly Ferry across the harbour to the city, acting like a tourist walking the streets, taking pictures under the famous Sydney Harbour Bridge and Opera House, visiting the casino, and of course enjoying many meals out and about with my mum.

Mum and I had always been foodies! But this time round it was nice to enjoy some foods that were part of my new routine, seeing that Sydney is one of the best cites in the world for all types of food, including healthy trendy cafes, vegan restaurants, juice bars, smoothie bowls, famers markets and all things I now loved! Gotta give it to you, Australia, out of the 44 countries I've been around the world, you really can't beat food in Australia. Some of the most amazing flavours, variety of all cuisines you could imagine and fresh produce making some of the most amazing creative dishes you can find! Probably why I was so overweight in the first place! LOL!

It's odd, it's like everything had changed in Sydney, but at the same time, nothing had. As I was walking abound Manly one day catching some time to myself, it's like I was walking through a time warp, or watching a video of my old paths. It's like the place was the same, the people, the culture, with just a few new buildings and shops popping up here and there that weren't there previously.

It really was a trip down memory lane of my entire first 24 or so years of my life before I had left. The beach I visited as a child, the old Manly Wharf and Waterworks Water Park we'd spent summer holidays at, the shop fronts facing the promenade with the cafes and restaurants we used to lounge at, the old Aqua Bar we tried to get in to as 16 and 17 years old, the street lining the beach front we used to zoom up and down cruising in our down up race cars, and the Corso with the famous Steyne Pub and Base Bar we went to every Friday and Saturday night without fail, in our early 20s partying till the sun came up over Manly Beach!

It's like I could see my entire life flashing before my eyes! To be honest, it was tripping me out a bit. Then here I was now, the new me in my old stomping ground. At that moment, I really was appreciative of every moment in my life, the good, the bad, the ugly. It really did shape me in to who I was and ultimately make me who I'd become today, and for that I was thankful, and I always will be. Never forget where you came from, no matter where that may be or what it may look like.

I think one of the other reasons I had put off coming back to Sydney for so long alone, was that what if I missed it here? What if I had a decision to make post-going back to the UK after the trip? The UK was my new comfort zone, my home now. But what if it made me want to come back to Sydney? I didn't know this place now…it wasn't me anymore.

But sure enough, Sydney will always be my first home and to me, it will always be there. "Australia ain't going anywhere, Carli," I said to myself, and in that moment, I knew the UK really was my new home.

I really had found myself there, and shed half myself there too! It would forever be my secondary home! I was content now, knowing I was exactly where I was meant to be with my life and just to keep going at it, as the best was yet to come!

Chapter 34
See Ya Later, Sydney!

The days were flying by in Sydney, as I knew they would and I was trying to see everyone I wanted to see, spend as much time as I could with my mum, again not knowing when the next opportunity would be to catch up and see her in person, but I vowed it wouldn't be this long next time!

Even though I loved my life in the UK, the one thing I would miss about Sydney is the weather and lifestyle! It's one thing I've always noticed to be very different in the UK. Sydney-siders (or all Aussies for that matter) really embrace the outdoors, all types of weather and really get out there, even on windy-cold days: rain, hail or shine, baby! Those Aussie babies are out there enjoying life! We will still be embracing it all, there smiling, saying, 'Oh, what a great day!' We just really know how to enjoy life, and I guess that is one characteristic I'll always appreciate I gained from growing up in Oz! I'm like this even in the UK on the coldest, wettest of days in winter! Always the silly Aussie wandering around with a big smile on my face, still saying, "What a great day!" when it's −1 degree outside!

I'd loved waking up to Manly Beach each day during my trip, being able to stroll down the streets, jogging along the promenade, having coffees watching all the surfers catching the waves and little 'nippers' getting their surf lifesaving lessons in. To this day, people still don't see how I choose to live in England, over this beautiful place, but I guess I never planned it that way. Life had taken me on a certain path I'd never expected, and I now had my reasons for loving it there too! Life has a funny way of choosing things for you sometimes.

When planning my return to Sydney earlier that year, one of my old school friends, the beautiful and talented Gemma, who had now started her own photography business, had reached out to me about doing a photo shoot. It was such a touching thought, as I had always been the girl carrying around disposable cameras at school capturing all our childhood memories that she would now love to return the favour and capture some shots of me in my current life as a new memory for me to have. I was so excited, and loved the concept, this would be the only shoot I'd done since my Sun article, so I couldn't wait.

We set off early one morning at sunrise, heading down to Shelly Beach, arms bundled with various outfits to choose from for the pictures. We shot about four or five looks including a daring red one piece, before I finally stripped off in to my birthday suit for a couple of artistic nude shots, half covered by the water. I didn't care who was around, as I saw a few surfers coming in off the break, I felt liberated in all my glory. After all, I'd been making alterations to my birthday suit for few years now, may as well show it off!

We had such a blast, and needless to say, the photos were amazing, Gem did such an amazing job, like no other photographer I know, this girl has a way with the lens and capturing you in your lifestyle. I will always be thankful to her for this, and it just gave me a greater taste for what I already knew, that I just wanted to keep doing work like this. I loved it, and felt in my element!

I had a few more days to go, doing last minute shopping, lunches, dinners and drinks with the girls, and then spending my last day with my mum getting our hair done and a final farewell dinner on the beach front; one of our favourite spots we used to always eat at together, before departing for the airport early the next morning.

Sure enough, it was as a teary goodbye as it was a hello just those few weeks earlier at Sydney Airport. Mum and I said our piece to each other, and I knew she was immensely proud of everything I had achieved, not just in body, but in mind, life and soul! She always had been proud of me, knowing I would always find my way and take care of myself, her 'Lil Miss Independent' as she always liked to call me. We had our final hugs and kisses before I began to walk through the departure doors, and as I took one last glance back over my shoulder, I could see her lovely face waving and blowing me kisses.

I can still see this image now in my mind. It seems to be a reoccurring scene for the two of us waving goodbye in airports, but I now had my life to live, and goals to go after, and with that in mind, I went through security and headed for my gate.

****

Wow, I thought to myself as I got on the plane and settled in my seat for the first leg of the long journey home, on to Dubai, then London. I couldn't believe it was over, after all this time! That wasn't so hard now, was it, Carli!

So much had changed, and yet, I was so complete and content with where I was with my life. Sometimes, you need to let go, like really let go of all your comfort zones and things you were made to know all your life, in order to really find yourself, even if that means leaving your only home you've ever known, your friends, your family!

It's like a saying I once saw on a meme, 'I always wonder why birds choose to stay in the same place when they can fly anywhere on Earth. Then I ask myself the same question about people'. and as the wheels took off from the tarmac, and we soared higher and higher in to the air, I was heading for the place I now called home, and I was happy knowing my wings were always in full flight ready to catch that bit of air to take me on to the next destination and part of my journey…

Chapter 35
Full Speed Ahead

I had vowed to myself in January that 2017 really was going to be my year—no, not one of those people that every year says 'New Year, New Me!' or sets resolutions for the sake of it, jumping on the bandwagon. This had to be it for me. I had spent enough time and years visualising, dreaming and planning out my ideas and goals. I had so much in my brain, all these plans and things I wanted to do, now I'd discovered my love for Health and fitness.

Like I always say you really should make your passion your pay check. So, that's exactly what I was going to do.

I was still working as a full-time recruiter, and despite loving that and helping people find jobs, I wanted to be helping myself to do MY dream job! That way, I could be helping more people in a different, healthier kind of way.

One of these days, I'm going to chuck it all in and resign as recruiter, that bit I knew for sure. I just had to get myself to that point and then would happily risk the career I'd known for over seven years to go out on my own working for my newly found passion. The day job was the last bit of my comfort zone; my financial stability really, as I was still living on my own, and having no one to lean on or fall back on I knew, I had to have a slight bit of structure to how I was going to take that big leap out of my 9–5 job!

I did have a real element of sensibility within me, and so I set out to really push forward this year with getting my website domain and business names brought, started working on future products and business ideas, looking in to trademarking, and registration—everything and anything that would help me go forward, you name it, I was researching and ticking it off my to-do-list! Everything I wanted to come to a reality in life! I had so, so many things I wanted to create: a business, a name for myself, this book, book two—yes, of course there is going to be more—recipes, clothes! *Why not?* I thought. *I want to turn this in to my business empire!*

Since I was a little girl, I had always dreamed about owning my own business, being my own boss, and for some reason, I always had an idea and vision the business would be something to do with myself, and quite literally, I would be the product—and sure enough, it was all happening before my very eyes!

My overall weight loss had started this journey, my transformation, my healthy lifestyle, and I wanted to use all of this experience and put it down in to products, services, books, tools and plans for others to use and be able to do the same. But not just as any old gimmick on the market or new fad coming out year on year, being endorsed by some celebrity to con you in to buying it. I wanted to create something great, something that actually would help people and really worked—for the long haul!

As I arrived back in the UK, I got to work, being as productive as I could possibly be. In May, I decided upon repeating a daily mantra that "The month of May was mine!" And every day that month, I committed to doing something every single day that would inevitably help me and my business goals come to life. And I did. I stuck to it, doing various tasks, networking, registering names, researching companies and competitors in the market. All this work. No matter how big or small the daily task was, it really was paying off. By the end of the month, I felt like I'd achieve more in those 30 days than I had in an entire year on my business plans.

Now, don't get me wrong, I had always been working on me, but me in body, weight loss, exercise related goals, and that was great as it gave me a steady head, and focus, but sometimes, with big weight loss achievements and maintaining, we can get a little wrapped up not wanting to be one of the many that fall off the wagon and pile it back on; there is that element of fear of going backwards, that we almost get so caught up (some say obsessed...I say passionate) with calories, what foods we can and can't eat, have we exercised enough today, and so on, and sometimes, we just need to take a step back and say, take a deep breath, and say yes, girl, you are doing OK! Keep reminding yourself, you've got this, be proud, you are still in your healthy state and life!

I had to now use everything I had achieved to really move forward with all the other plans that my new healthy life could create for me and ultimately for others too. Goals don't create themselves you know, you have to! And boy, did I know that was true!

So, I decided to continue my new mantra, and every day this year, I had to do something for me, my business or a goal, even if it was something very small, whether it be write a page in this book, connect and network with someone I already knew or meet someone new, research something I needed to further myself and plans, look in to courses that would help me grow and gain knowledge, whatever it may be; every-single-day, I was doing something, something for me!

If you want something in life, you really, really have to work, work, work at it! And so I did, and every day, I could really feel I was getting one step closer and closer. And just like with weight loss, these things don't happen overnight, small incremental steps, add up over time, to exactly what it is you want!

Chapter 36
Lights, Camera, Action!

As I adopted this positive proactive attitude, I could really see all the plans I'd written down and been visualising in my head starting to shape together and come to life. I felt like I was really getting somewhere, even if they were baby steps.

I had really put myself out there this year to meet people, network and go to new events. My theory is that people aren't going to just walk on up to your door, knock and say, "Hi, I'm blah blah blah and I want to help you!" So stop thinking that is going to happen and go out there and make it happen for yourself. You may not realise it at that exact moment, but often certain people or encounters you come across may lead to something later on, that might not have otherwise, should you have not done that thing at that exact moment! Just trust in the process, okay!

The fitness expo season was kicking off for 2017 in the UK and that meant the line-up of some of the biggest expos in Europe, as well as some smaller niche start-up ones, which I made the conscious decision to go to all of them. I felt that if I wanted to really make a name for myself in the industry, I had to go out there, see the market for what it was, my competition so to speak (even though to me it's not competition, I'm genuinely happy for everyone's success and different stories, there is room for us all, everyone has something different to offer the wider public). I wanted to see what were the latest trends, what were people in to at the moment? I had to do my research and absorb myself in this world if I really wanted to be a part of it.

Through doing so, I found that despite the ever-growing saturated fitness market not just in the UK but around the world, my story was still quite niche and unique in a way.

Don't get me wrong, I know there are lots of weight loss stories everyday popping up in magazine and on social media every week, but I still felt like there was something different about me and my journey, that no big fitness icon out there at the moment had done what I had done personally.

Like you had Dana Lynn Bailey, Michelle Lewin, Kai Green, Emily Skye, Kayla, Joe Wicks, Simone Panda and the likes, these types of fitness type icons were all over the world where ever you turned, but I thought I really wanted to be that icon of a long-lasting weight loss success story, and go on to help people do the same.

With fat and obesity being one of the worst health problems in the world today, I felt there really was a massive gap in the market, and I wanted to be the one to fill it! The best bit was I believed I really could, if I kept my mind to it and really worked even harder on getting these business goals up and running and sharing my story wider than just through social media channels, then why not, hey! I felt I had so much to give and share with others, and I could feel there were so many people wanting this real, honest kind of help as well.

It was around this time that I realised I really wanted to help tackle the obesity and health crisis the world over, and go further than skin deep with it, really getting to the root cause of the problems and of course giving these people long lasting ways that work.

So, almost every week for a month, I was travelling about visiting various expos and fitness events, including BodyPower Expo one of the most well-known across Europe spread over three days in Birmingham which is one of the biggest and best in terms of brands, bodybuilding, global fitness icons, supplements stalls, (and generally young guys walking around without shirts on, having an ab-off between themselves, even if they don't even realise it…)

Jokes aside, it's still a great weekend to attend if you have never been before, it's an eye open, and one of the first I ever went to back in 2015, returning every year since. I'll always love all the hustle and bustle, countless protein brands and samples, muscles everywhere you look and generally anyone and everyone interested in anything fitness related! It's a great atmosphere to be a part of.

Alongside that, I also attended BeFit, an ever-growing event especially in women's fitness, as well as FitCon and Balance, two relatively new expos on the scene. And these were the ones that really paid off for me, meeting some people that would later lead to other opportunities, contacts and general information, I would have maybe never come across should I had not gone to these events. So, one thing I really took away from this was that you really have to put yourself out there, go on your own if you have to, talk to people, learn, grow and share knowledge between you. It's the only way to evolve beyond what you are, or should I say what you were, your former self.

It made me realise you can always find an open door and the answer to your questions if you really want to. You just have to seek out the right people or scenarios to gain the answers. It showed me how lovely some people were, genuinely interested in my story, and wanting to help me succeed in sharing it as far as possible, and doing this all from the kindness of their hearts because they too saw my vision. I felt truly grateful, and so happy, it was like they could see the images in my head that I had for myself, and could also picture my goals for what they were to become soon enough. I was genuinely so thankful for these kinds of people and truly humbled that they could see what I was seeing, even before it was a reality.

It's like sometimes I would tell people my story, and they would just stare at me blankly and say, "But yeah, what can you do with it now, how can you make something from that story?" And I realised that was the difference, some people see a way to make it work, and see potential, full flight with you and your goals, and some people see brick walls. It's like that saying that used to be all over Instagram or Facebook: "Have goals so big, you feel uncomfortable telling small minded people." That is how I felt sometimes often meeting friends of friends or going on first dates with people who didn't know me and sharing or confiding in them about my journey and aspirations; some would get it and some just wouldn't. But I could often sense the achievers and dreamers from the ones that just couldn't see past mundane routine life, and choose not to go to deep with them on what I had planned for my future. I'd just let them see it one day, that was easier.

I chose to spend my time more around people that had drive, ambition and generally a positive outlook on life, these people have better energy and create better vibes, rather than energy suckers who drain you. I really can't deal with being around people who are negative or whinge all the time, it's too exhausting. And I ain't got time for that—ain't no one got time for that!

So, I continued to interact with the good kinds of people, networking, making friends and potential business opportunities, growing that circle!

One of those people happened to be a guy named Denz. We came across each other not long after FitCon through Instagram, as we seemed to know a few of the same people from the fitness world. Denz was on his own path and journey of following his goals and aspirations in the creative film and videography world.

See, for me, it's not about just meeting people exactly like you, having the exact same goals or journey. For me, it's about meeting someone who is going for their full potential and dreams in their own chosen field, whatever that may be, and how we can connect and bring those two sets of dreams and passions together to create something, utilising both our skill sets and experiences.

It was around the time I'd realised I really needed to get going on my YouTube and grow that alongside my Instagram page. I'd started my YouTube almost seven months earlier at the end of 2016, but hadn't put that much effort in to it, as the videoing and editing game was proving it needed more time and skills than I may have had, and even thought I could do a mediocre job at it. I don't half-ass anything in my life, I like things to look good, and be quality! So, that's where Denz came in. He reached out to me on Instagram and we hit it off, talking as if we had known each other for years. I shared with Denz some of my ideas, current plans for YouTube and also some big future plans that I saw myself doing within the years to come. The best bit about it all was that Denz could see and feel it too. He got what I wanted to do now and long-term and was keen to be part of it, and I knew I wanted him to be too. Some people just get you, and you know when you meet them, they are the man (or woman) for the job!

I had explained to Denz I had been wanting to do a series of YouTube videos of workouts for each body part, incorporating all the exercises I did in the early days of my journey as a 'beginner' as this was something my followers had been asking for.

One of my worst problem areas, that so many people asked me for tips on was my arms, so we decided to start with that body part as my first video tutorial for people to follow along with either at home or in the gym. Now, all we needed was a venue to film in. So, I reached out to my friend Mickey who worked at Fitness First and we were able to use the gym at a quiet period in the day as they had a great little studio room we could utilise for the filming.

Denz and I met for the first time that afternoon, feeling like we were old pals by now! When you share so much of your journey with someone and learn about theirs, connecting through your passions, it's almost natural when you met, it's like we had been filming together for years!

We were buzzing at the thought of both our goals coming together and really seeing it in to reality! We quickly got to work on the plan for the shoot, what we wanted in each shot, the exercises, audio, demos etc…and within an hour, we'd almost shot the full thing, 10 various exercises to work those bingo wings!

It felt so natural like I'd been doing fitness videos for a long time now. I just loved it, I was over the moon, seeing another idea I'd had, albeit it amateur videos, coming to life. I knew this was almost like a practice for the real thing one day! I'd shared with Denz about really making a professional set of work-out DVDS one day, in this format. So, this was like a trial to the public, see how followers responded and really learn what worked and didn't work. I guess you could say this was almost like the dress rehearsal knowing one day I would have a full box set of exercise DVDs to buy! (Yes, watch this space, they will happen.) See, you have to have full faith in everything you want to do, and I knew one day I would make them!

Denz and I had a brilliant afternoon; the energy was crazy, we were both on a high, cloud nine! See, when you do what you love, it really doesn't feel like work! We were already planning the next one and when we could meet up again to film!

Over the next week, Denz went to town on the videography, creative elements and editing of the short workout, to produce my first mini amateur workout. Despite a few bloopers, and learning curves with the sound, I put it out on my Instagram and YouTube channel *MissCarliJay HealthyLiving* with an overwhelming response from new and old followers. Their comments were great. For once, it wasn't one of these unrealistic celebrity DVDs like 'Get a bum in five mins' or 'Tone your abs with these five workouts'. It was real, it was all the exercises I had actually done for months on end, first in my lounge room at home with cheap old weights off eBay, then in the gym progressing on to larger weights, helping to lose fat, tone my shape and skin and build muscle. I was no expert or lifelong PT, I was just a girl who had educated myself on what worked for me, playing around with various exercise routines and literally the proof was in the pudding!

This was then just the start, the next video we made was an intermediate version of the arm workout, so people didn't give up or get bored, but once they were comfortable with the beginners set that they had something new to go to next and keep at it, getting fitter, stronger and of course more confident in the gym. As that's one thing I really wanted to instil with my followers, as so many said they had confidence issues going to the gym altogether, let alone stepping foot in the weights room. So, I was happy that I was able to share and provide encouragement to anyone feeling that way, along with my some of my other followers who were regular gym goers!

I knew I had to now keep these videos going and creating new content, not just exercise videos. So, this was just the beginning of filming YouTube content! I knew I had so many more ideas and with my creative juices going full steam ahead, this was just the start of what I wanted to create joining up with others putting passions together!

Returning to Sydney, 2017; Mum and I at the Sydney Harbour Bridge

Mum and I at Manly Beach, 2017

My photoshoot at Manly Beach. *Photo Credit "Gemma Peanut"*

Paddle-boarding in the River Thames, 2017

Refresh Festival – talking on the Body Confidence Panel, 2017

At Be:Fit Festival London, 2017

Making my first workout video for YouTube, 2017

Ice Skating in London, Christmas 2017

Chapter 37
Body Confidence

As the months were flying on by, it was important for me to keep putting myself out there, never wanting to get too comfortable, pursuing new avenues, growing, trying new things and continuing to meet people from all walks of life who were following their own passions and aspirations. It's like putting together a sports team, everyone has a position to play, their individual role, and when you get everyone together, team work really does make the dream work!

With everyone I was meeting, we connected in some way, and the building blocks were forming, helping us push each other forward, and further up the ladder in our own fields.

I'd met some great people in PR, journalists, photographers, others developing recipe books or supplement products, as well as some professional athletes charging ahead for their goals. This made me want to go bigger and better, it's like how they say you are the company you keep, so it does benefit to have a circle of positive people that are also wanting to succeed and win at their own game too. You really do lift each other higher.

It was during the summer after going to all those expos and meeting different people, that one of my next goals came true. I was approached by a start-up events and production company who were launching a new fitness and health expo in the UK called 'Refresh Festival'. This was to be a two-day outdoor festival with all things healthy and fitness lifestyle related with loads of food stands, clothing, brands, activities and talks hosted by the Great British Athlete and Olympian Dame Kelly Holmes. The production team asked if I would like to join a women's panel talking on 'Body Confidence' and the impact this topic had from social media.

I was over the moon, and of course I said yes! This was a topic I was very passionate about, especially in today's world, with the ever-growing world of social media, reality stars, celebrities everywhere you turn, being very impressionable on our young adults and teens, both men and women, and the pressure to look good. I was so supportive of this, as for someone who was once 127 kg and confident as hell both then and now, I wanted to be able to share some of my tips on this in the hope to get at least one person to be more confident about themselves and their own body no matter what shape or size.

As the festival weekend arrived in September, I headed out to Hampshire with a few friends and, of course, Denz to film and vlog the day for YouTube.

The weather was perfect and the vibe was great around the event with loads of activities going on, fitness enthusiasts enjoying the classes, food samples and people generally enjoying themselves soaking up the atmosphere.

As the time slot for our women's panel arrived for us to hit the stage, I was more excited with anticipation rather than nerves. I'd always loved talking in front of crowds and engaging with wider audiences so couldn't wait to get up there. As we got going the panel was introduced one by one then we went straight in to questions all giving our opinions and answers, and I could feel my smile beaming as I was just so happy to be part of this important topic.

For me, I really wanted to instil in people how important it is to have self-love and ultimately create this level of confidence from within. Everything in life stems from within; our behaviours, fears, perceptions of ourselves and one another, confidence, issues etc...and often with how much reality TV, social media, magazines, fashion adverts we have around us in everyday life, everywhere we turn, people are comparing themselves to the next girl, or being shown unrealistic images or ways of life through marketing companies tactics.

But not everyone in the world is the same, and we have to accept we are who we are. Yes, it's OK to want to change things about yourself, but do it for the right reasons, do it for you. Not because you want to be like someone else, or because you are self-hating.

You need to have confidence in who you are on the inside and out, and be confident in your own abilities in this moment now. Don't doubt yourself but instead, be proud. You are a once in a life time person, there is no one like you, and we only get one lifetime to prove it. So, don't doubt yourself. Love who you are, whole heartedly. And when you love who you are on the inside—heart, mind and soul, you also have to love what you are on the outside; have that all over body confidence no matter what you see in the mirror—this is you now!

We are who we are, and even if you want to alter things about yourself, that's OK, but you need to love who you are now, first, before you make changes, then only then can you start to change things about yourself for a healthier, fitter, better you. It's about being your best self.

Stop worrying what someone else is doing with their life, that's wasted energy you could better spend on, like on you! You have to be positive about you and the things you want to do! That will create happiness within, and when you're happy inside, it will radiate out. You'll start to feel good all over! Each day, wake up and be thankful and grateful for who you are, acknowledge something different each day that you love about yourself. We should be thankful for what we are and what we can become with a strong body, mind and a heart full of self-love! It's very easy for us to compliment others, but do you ever just look in the mirror and compliment yourself? If not, why? Be kind to yourself and shower yourself with compliments too.

So, in summary, what I'm trying to say here is, be confident with the body you see in front of you, and learn to love it as is. Then only then, it's OK if there are things you want to change and alter that birthday suit of yours, but do that for you, because you want to become a better, healthier, fitter version of the you, you see staring back at you in the mirror!

Create your best self, inside and out, and if you do decide to make changes, enjoy the process and journey you go on, learning about yourself and getting to know yourself on a different level!

**

The rest of the expo was an overall great experience, we all had such a good time, and I was so excited to see all the footage Denz captured, and of course soon enough, he put it all together for me and I had my very first expo vlog! Slowly and surely, each part of my journey was coming together, getting more exposure, sharing my story across different platforms and pushing ahead with creating a name and business for myself.

Chapter 38
Give It a Go

During all these months, alongside working the day job and pursuing my hobby trying to turn it in to a business venture, I was still training every day, enjoying incorporating anything active in to my routine, and still practising all those good habits I'd introduced as part of my healthy lifestyle.

But some days, it came more naturally than others, you know I should be used to this all by now, but others days, I did have to give myself just a little poke, you know, keeping on the chosen path, as a gentle reminder. We, as humans, can become complacent at times, so it's important to remember to always keep yourself on your toes, mixing it up from time to time. If not, we can become stagnant, even at the good things in life and return in to a comfort zone (and we all know, no change happens in a comfort zone). It's like I'd reached a peak of almost doing too much, really pushing myself to keep at it, like a mouse on a wheel: don't stop, don't stop, don't stop! That gym, work, gym, sleep, eat, repeat life. I really, really just wanted to get to my goals and achieve everything I had planned.

But even though I was being so productive, keeping myself busy, working on me, and never even thinking about giving up, it's like I had reached a bit of a 'slump' so to speak.

Like with weight loss, when working away and seeing results, it keeps you going, but when you stop seeing physical results, even though you still may be improving, this is where people can lose their motivation to keep at it and get fed up, irritated, and slowly do less and less. I guess you can say this is slightly similar to where my life and business goals had reached a point during 2017, I was working away on everything every day, but not necessarily seeing the rewards just yet for all the effort. But I was quick to recognise this hurdle and not fall victim to it, just like I had during my weight loss journey.

It is hard working away every day, knowing you are doing stuff to get you there, making sacrifices, working endless hours, going through stints of anxiety, battling with yourself mentally on occasions. But you just have to know it will all pay off one day, you really have to know that. I guess it is hard when there really is no end date, but you have to really believe it will all come together, and just trust in the process, trust in the universe, and ultimately, trust in yourself and all your abilities!

Positivity is definitely one of my best strengths, it always has been. I always see the best in everything, never one to be optimistic or negative in the slightest, so I just had to keep visualising what I was working for even though I couldn't see it in real life or touch it just yet. I was manifesting it through my hard work and really practising and having faith in the law of attraction, that never giving up mentality, pep talks to myself on the daily!

Someone once said to me it can be a lonely ride to the top when you are working on your own goals, and I really do see what they meant now. So, this is why I think it's doubly as important to have a very good relationship with yourself, seek guidance from within, have that all over confidence, a very strong mentality and enjoy learning about yourself, your mind and body! Enjoy spending time with yourself, being independent, appreciating your space, because yes, times can be tough, I'm not going to deny that, and sometimes, all you have is yourself to rely on, it's how you get through it, 'cause you will, and that's what counts.

At the end of the day, you are the only one that can see everything you want, and you are the only one you can always count on, you may have support and encouragement from others if you have a good support network, but ultimately, it is down to you. So, stay strong and always keep your mind-set in check on where you are heading in the life you want to live.

One way I really tried to do this, throughout this year in particular, was to try anything and everything I'd ever wanted to do, you know to still have fun with my healthy life, self-discovery keeping active all in one.

You know those ideas you come up with, or you see something on TV and say, "Oh, I've always wanted to try that..." Yeah well, I went to town on trying all the new things I came across. And this was definitely one way to mix it up, keeping out of the slump, staying motivated, and not getting complacent or bored. Yep, my life was anything but boring at the moment! I was literally jumping from one activity to the next!

I started off making a list of all the random activities I had always wanted to try (and I mean all the non-conventional ones) not like going for a walk or a swim...my list was:

- Stand-up paddle board,
- Rock climb,
- Bikram and Kundalini Yoga,
- Aerial fitness, yoga slings and hoops,
- Trapeze,
- Ice skate more often,
- Horse ride again,
- Try salsa classes and Latin dance

The list went on, anything and everything I came across that I wanted to try, saw in a magazine, in a movie, on Instagram, it went on my 'give-it-a-go' list!

And every month, or almost every couple of weeks, I was ticking one of the list. The ones that I enjoyed, were easily added to my permanent routine, or ones that had classes near me I stuck to and added them to my weekly workout schedule, and some of them were more one-off classes I attended when I could.

I was loving it, I wasn't waiting for others to join me or getting a group together and organising it, it was just me, getting up and getting moving, anyway I could. It sure was a fun positive way of getting to know myself on an even deeper level and staying motivated. I know for me being independent and used to being on my own, these tasks were easy, but I know some of my girlfriends couldn't even stand to go to the mall shopping or eat on their own, so these tasks may sound daunting to some people, but trust me, start small and go to one class or activity by yourself, and just let yourself go; it really is liberating! Don't be shy, embarrassed or self-conscious, just enjoy it for you!

One of my favourite activities that I had been dying to do again since visiting the Dominican Republic two years prior, was paddle boarding, and now I was half the size, so I'm sure I would pick it up easily after all this time! But everyone kept saying to me, "You live in the UK, you're not on the beaches of Oz anymore Carli, how can you paddle board? ...And if you know me well, to me that's a challenge—accepted! I don't like being told I can't do something, when if you just think outside the box, you damn well can!

So, sure enough, I went to trusty old Google and searched about Stand up Paddle Boarding (SUP) in the UK, and sure enough, there were a few spots around you could do it, mainly on the coast at holiday and caravan sites, but I was surprised to see there were a few nearer to London! Yes, in the River Thames there were a few schools and clubs you could rent boards from and have lessons.

But I wanted my own, and I'd seen people kayaking and canoeing in the river near where I lived in Surrey, so thought, why don't I just get a board and go out on my own! And sure enough, I did. I brought a 10-foot inflatable board with paddle and pump and within a matter of days it was starting to heat up in the UK as the summer drew closer. Lucky for me, we were having a rare early 'heat wave' as the Brits like to call it the moment it went over 25 degrees Celsius LOL. So, I headed down to the river near Walton-on-Thames Bridge where I'd seen many a boats, rowers and kayaks entering the water. I parked up, unloaded my equipment and board and began to pump away, inflating my board, which was surprisingly very sturdy! Once fully inflated, I picked up the 10-foot board (about double my height) under one arm, paddle in the other and walked confidently over to the boat ramp in my black one piece and straight in to the River Thames. I wadded at first feeling the cool water then slowly kneeled on to the board...

As I steadied myself there on my knees, I was so excited, I thought I'm really doing this, and without a second thought, I got to my feet, then I just stood there loud and proud balancing myself, using the paddle for support as the fisherman on the shoreline watched on, probably thinking who is this bloody crazy girl in a swimming costume in the middle of the Thames!

Without another glance at the shore line, I swiftly took off, sticking to the banks, taking it easy until I got the swing of it again, and within 10–15 minutes, it felt so natural. I was easily swinging the oar from side to side, paddling away like a pro! *Why don't more people do this?* I thought. Sure enough, I got plenty of commentary and questions from the residents along the water front, or families with their kiddies feeding bread to the swans and ducks, asking me about it, how many lessons do you need, had I fallen in, what was it like etc...etc...and I've got to say, it really is easier than it looks, just have confidence, take it easy and most importantly, just give it a go!

Over the summer, I was going practically every day, and over the months, I only managed to fall in the Thames once, keeping my mouth firmly shut when I did, not catching any bugs despite all the stories you hear about the Thames water. By the end of the summer, about 10 other local people I'd made friends with on the water had too brought boards and were giving it a go, including one 70-year-old couple! Sometimes that is all people need: the encouragement of someone else doing something, to say, "Hey, they're doing it, let's try that too!" So, the more we all get out there and think outside the box, the more active we can be together.

I think this ultimately was one of the best summers I've ever had in my seven years in the UK. You can really say I made the most of it and the weather we have it, for all I know I could have been in LA as I was motoring down the river. You just have to appreciate what you have around you! So, when people still say to me, "Oh, don't you miss the weather in Sydney? What are you doing here?" I can simply say, "Nah, the weather is great here." (It's just how you use it and adapt to what you can do with it.)

As the summer came to an end and it was starting to get too cold to board in my swimsuit, I could have brought a wetsuit, but I thought best save it for next year, that way I won't get bored of it and have it to look forward to again. So, I packed away the board as the winter months were approaching and decided it was time to try a new activity for this season coming!

I'd always enjoyed stretching, Pilates and beginners Yoga tutorials on YouTube, doing it in my own home, but I'd always had a great interest in learning about Yoga, its history, benefits and what you can gain from it, especially hot Yoga, known as Bikram. So, off I set to find a studio to practice and for the first time in my life, take part in a class style workout (I'd never been one for classes previously, always working out alone or 1–2–1 with a friend).

Boy am I glad I did choose this as the next sport to try, as the yoga really was one I felt I connected with the most, as for me it's deeper than just the movements and exercise, it's more about what is going on in the inside, balancing your energies, relaxation and a way of rejuvenating. Since I was young, I'd always had an interest in holistic therapies, spirituality and connecting with yourself in a different way, so Yoga really did resonate with me and I started going 4–5 times a week as I was finding its benefits were too great not to miss. It was really helping me focus, be un-apologetically myself, and find what I was searching for on a higher level. It was a chance to be away from the world, be at one with myself, and be right there living in that moment for the 60–90 minute yoga sessions I was partaking in. Alongside practising meditation at home daily, as I felt the two really went hand in hand and complimented each other with joint benefits.

And see, here is my main point with all this stuff, if I'd never put myself out there and tried it, I never would have found that clarity or pure enjoyment from these activities and new-found hobbies.

So, always put yourself out there and give things a go, even if you only try something once, at least you did it, as it's better than having not tried it at all, and never knowing. Don't wait for someone to ask you to go to a class or sport, just do it! This is what will really keep you going, finding things you enjoy, spending time with yourself and learning about you and your new-found strengths and interests, experiencing the benefits, and then seeing the benefits in your everyday way of life working for you.

Chapter 39
Change

I was having a fantastic year, I knew myself now, better than I ever had, I was exactly what I wanted to be, no questions asked, and I knew where I was heading, all with a smile on my face every single day!

I'd been through such a 360 in my life, all stemming from that one original decision to change my life for a healthier me!

I could have never imaged back on that day in 2014, everything that has now come from that decision to get healthy and lose weight. Sometimes, one decision really can change more than you ever expected. And in that case, that is surely true for me.

That's why I'm glad I never thought of it just as weight loss, instead I had always thought of it this time round as a lifestyle change, as wellness, and a complete overhaul of me. When you see it as that, I do really believe you have a better chance of sticking with it and succeeding, and that is why I wanted to share with you everything that's changed for me, not just the physical weight and how I look, it was all actually about the aftermath and the good repercussions that came from that initial action to become a healthier, fitter version of myself.

When really wanting to change who you are on the inside and out, you have to look at all the facts around you and your environment, because if you don't change them as well, you won't flourish permanently. You may change for the moment, but then you are still in the same old environment and atmosphere, and those bad habits, people, bad energies, same old routines will still be there...so really you changed nothing that surrounds you, and that's where I feel so many people fall back in to old ways and their old selves.

You have to really be prepared to change! I mean change everything! You, your surroundings, your routine, your comfort zone—your life—YOU. Yep, change it ALL!

I hope now you see the real underlying message of this entire book, and ultimately, my story.

You probably picked up this book to start with because you've always wanted to lose weight, struggled with your size, and potentially found nothing that worked...or maybe, you wanted tips on getting fit and healthy...and yes, this book is all about that too obviously, that's what started it all. But now that you've got to this part in my story, I hope you see what it's also really been about, and how to get success and long-lasting results in all things you do in your life.

This book is also about finding your true self, your relationship with who you are and being absolutely 'you'. Because that's what I find holds a lot of people back, not just from a weight loss goal, but from any goal in life. People are not willing to wholeheartedly be themselves, not going after what they really, really want in life. Maybe through fear, or what others will judge them for, or simply not believing it's all possible, and thinking it's too hard before they've even tried.

So yes, it's about weight loss and body goals, being fit and healthy, sticking to your new healthy life, and motivating yourself no matter what the body goal is…but it's about that whole process of getting there, finding yourself, liberating yourself, and what you do with that once you've got there.

And once you're there, you realise you've gone and done something for you! Ultimately, you! Not for your children, not for a boyfriend, not for your mum, no, you've gone and done this 100% for yourself. You've gone and made yourself the best you, you could possibly be—and that's liberating in itself, like a sense of euphoria! That for me was my big 'WOW' moment—like I can achieve any body goal I want, but not only that, I can now achieve anything in life, it's all about that inner belief, with no limitations what-so-ever!

So, I truly believe when you nurture yourself and take care of your overall well-being in the best way you possibly can, no excuses, making yourself a priority to be so healthy, you are liberating yourself for life, to be able to go on and do anything you want. And that's what I wanted to show people. It wasn't just to inspire people to lose weight, or build muscle, or get active, but it was to inspire people to go and be whoever they want to be, life is too short! So go after your best self and your best life, that's what we were put on this earth for. A-once-in a-lifetime kinda deal, this is not a dress rehearsal!

See, with losing the weight and getting healthy, I ultimately created my best self, and then along with my best self came such fire, passion and determination to go for my best life, and then the desire to go for everything I've always wanted. It's like I was stronger in more ways than one now, and I had all the motivation I needed to go for it all.

Life really is what you make it, and we are here one time only, so I wanted to encourage everyone to create who they want to be, own it, be unapologetically yourself, as long as you are doing good and not harming anyone or anything, then don't worry what people think of you or your aspirations, don't wait for it, go for it! Find what it is you want, and you will have your true happiness within, and trust me, that will radiate out.

****

As the year of 2017 was coming to a close, I'd had a couple more articles go out in Women's Health in the US and New Idea Magazine in Australia. My Instagram presence was growing, I'd put plans together to get my website up and running, and I was working on my clothing brand. Smiling to myself, I thought, *It really all was coming together.*

And as I sit here on a very cold wintery afternoon in Costa typing away, I can't help but think what's next for me? But I guess that's the beauty of it all. If you had asked me that four years ago, I could have said some mundane answer, as back then I had no idea where I was heading. But now, I have an idea, I have a plan, I can't say exactly where I will be in 4–5 years' time, but I have a damn good idea of roughly what I want and where I want to be, and this time. I know how to create it and get there. I'm now built for this, mentally! Mentally ready to go forward and achieve whatever I set my mind to!

Chapter 40
The Grand Finale

Even before I was close to finishing this book, I kept thinking and worrying about what will be my ending...how will it end...what will happen... I generally had no idea how to end this book. I struggled, racking my brain for a while on how to finish it...

But then realised my journey is never ending, no finish date, the healthy life is just that, an ongoing lifestyle, so it will never end for me. And so, really, the ending needed to just create itself. I needed to just make it happen. Take that plunge. I had to tell myself just to go for it! Like I've been telling you all to do with your goals, and I really had to take my own advice here and make the ending just happen!

So, as I type this last chapter of my book today, I decided I will be making this goal become a reality. *This is what's next for me,* I thought. I will be ending this year and kicking off 2018 seeking out a literary agent and book publisher over the coming weeks, so that one day you will be reading this, and I hope you reading this will lead you to taking the first steps in changing your lifestyle for the better or maybe you have already began...

Maybe you are reading this as you cycle away on your new home exercise bike, or maybe your sitting pool side reading this as your holiday novel or perhaps you're on the train on the way to work, or maybe just curled up on the couch having a bit of rest and relaxation afternoon. Whatever it is, I hope you've enjoyed it, and can take something away from my story no matter what age you are, if you're male or female, and especially no matter what size you are, I hope there is something in this book that can push you forward to your best self!

So, if you are sitting there now holding your copy, reading this then just know I found that ending I was looking for, and as I type the last words of this book, then also know this was all incredibly worth it for me; all the changes and sacrifices have all paid off. So, never be scared to take that risk and go for what it is you really want in life, no matter the goal or end prize. Nothing is too big or too small to achieve if you want it bad enough and are willing to do everything you can for it, so just keep remembering you too can have it all!

I'll be damned if you ever let anyone tell you it can't be done, because I hope by now you've realised everything you want is possible with the right mentality and attitude!

I'm not going to finish this with 'the end' as this is just the start of my story and I know I will be sharing a whole lot more with you all very soon. So, for now, I will say thank you! Thank you for reading this, and thank you for being part of my journey as each and every single one of you reading this now is. So, it's not goodbye, it's a see you soon!

Acknowledgements

Thank You to the Moon and Back

I want to start these thanks to all the people who have supported me who I have never even met, my followers, you reading this now, the people who watch my YouTube videos, the subscribers, yep, all of you! Thank you! Because without every single one of you, I wouldn't have been able to share my story as far as I have. You have all helped me, spurring me on to continue with my own goals, and in turn, I hope I've been able to return the favour for you all to go achieve yours! It's very powerful the way we can all connect in this day and age through social media platforms around the globe, and I'll always be thankful for this, and trust me, it doesn't go unnoticed! If I could hug every single one of you, god damn, I would!

To all the people I've met along my journey, in the gyms, expos, fitness festivals, you've also all been part of this and made it what it is, adding to my journey and experiences!

To all the journalists, PR reps and magazine editors that have helped me share my journey both near and far in print and online, thank you for showing an interest and publishing my story and articles. With a special thank you to Laura Quick and Rachel Chatham for always going that extra mile and reaching out to me.

To my publishers Austin Macauley for taking a chance on a 'yet to be discovered' author, thank you to all the teams who have been involved in making this book come to life with a massive thank you to the Production and Editorial teams, Graphics department, and Marketing team, as well as a special mention to Vinh Tran, Simon Potter, James Amstell and Chris Lee for all your help over the months and the time you have all put in at Austin Macauley to make this book the finished article that it is today for the readers.

To all the friends I've trained with, spending countless hours with me in various gyms around the country—thank you! Every session has been unique in some way, and I took away more from it than you probably realised at the time.

To all my previous colleagues, employers, managers and work places—thanks for putting up with my endless hours of chat about fitness, health, food and weight loss! For being so good to me through my journey and enabling me to have it all and pursue my hobby whilst keeping up a full-time job! To my fitfam here in the UK, you've all been amazing in your own ways, sharing your journeys with me and being part of the start of my fitness experience, to which I'll never forget and I'll always be thankful for—to Manny, Ash, Lydia, Shanaz, Moses, Tanya, Nat, Glaston, Locksmith, Mubz, Andrea, Charles, Sharah, Daniel B and Micquel for your love, friendship and support along the way—thank you all!

To Denz and Emily T, thank you for showing an interest and both wanting to work with me, collaborating using all our passions to create some amazing work and bring each of our ideas to life. I will never forget you both for being part of this in your own ways, and I will forever be grateful for your big hearts and beautiful creative minds! Thank you.

To all my beautiful girlfriends and to my amazing guy mates who are like brothers to me, both here in the UK and in Australia, both new and old, there are so many of you to list but you know who you all are! You've all known me in different ways and in different stages of my life—whether it be in junior or high school, my late teens and 20's hanging out on the Northern Beaches, or my days here in the UK. Thank you for always letting me be me, I've never conformed or been one to stay still, or be how people expect me to be, and you've taken me for who I am in all my glory, odd ways, direct speech, 'say it how it is' type of ways. I've got so much love for you all and will always be here for each and every single one of you, and I want you to know you're more to me than family and I'll always appreciate every single one of you and the times we have shared, so to all of you thank you, and with a special mention to Skye, Andrea, Tracy K, Laura F, Pip, Emma C, Justin S, Ade W, Athan, Geoff, Aurora, Caz, Shannon, Bianca, Annie, Jess D, Candice, Gemma, Elke, Alison G, Juz, Erin, Catherine R and Katherine O.

To TJ for being like family to me and always being there through my health journey as one of my biggest supporters and friend, that will always mean the world to me. To Leon McKenzie, Del Aruofor, Dominic Hay, Lee Akpareva for your friendship and support over the years and words of wisdom. To Michael Essien for your friendship, support and always encouraging me to go further and remain my positive self, I'll forever appreciate this. To AJ for being there for me on more occasions than you probably realise, on the days that were tougher than others your presence was always appreciated, and thank you for taking me as I was at all stages of my journey both big and small and accepting me for who I was. To Joey 'dizzle' Duncan, we sure have come a long way since we were 17 growing up on the Northern Beaches of Sydney, I'll always be so grateful we met and have kept in contact all these years, your never ending support will never go unnoticed. Thank you to all of you!

To Emma, Cheryl & Emily—where do I start! You three have been like rocks through my life over the years and each played a special part and supported me through various stages of my growth! Emma, we've know each other since we were 12 and you've always been like a sister to me, I know we can both call on each other for anything and we would be there in a heartbeat! Em and Chez—boy am I one lucky girl to not just have found one amazing girlfriend in the UK but to be blessed with you both beautiful souls! You are all so unique, and I am so blessed to call you friends, and will always appreciate all the support you've given me. You three are beyond amazing and I can't even put it in to words in this paragraph how truly grateful I am, you all have done more for me than you know! So much love for ya, girlies! Thank you!

To my mum, thank you for everything you were to me growing up, everything you are now and everything that you will always be to me. You truly are amazing and whether you know it or not, your experiences guided me. They showed me what I wanted and didn't want in life. Your big kind heart, caring nature and funny quirky traits will always be things I love about you. I know some things in this book you may have been anxious to read or shocked, but I hope you understand why I had to write everything I did. You know I'm real and opinionated, and have always done things my way, so this book would never have been anything but that either. Thank you for always supporting me and encouraging me, even through my rebellious teenage days and early 20s, as well as being there for me on the other side of the world. You really are the best! Love you lots, Susie-Q!

And lastly to me...this book is almost a dedication to myself for what I've achieved. Thank you for never giving up on yourself, always being faithful to your goals, always being your number one supporter, being there for yourself no matter what, even when no one else was, through the toughest darkest days. Knowing I had the courage and perseverance, not just to lose weight but to achieve life-long goals, business goals, financial goals and to be unapologetically yourself whilst doing so. Thank you. Thank you for always being you, staying true to that, being positive and happy throughout, and going after all you desire without a second thought...thank YOU! xxx

Thank You Everyone, Much Love, Peace and Good Vibes, Always xxx

Extra Pages for the Reader
Summary Goals and Tips

Ask yourself, why are you doing this? Yes, it may be partly for your children, or your partner etc, but ultimately, you have to want to do this for yourself. You have to see the true value in wanting to do it and find the motivation from within yourself of what this means to you.

If you don't actually want to succeed in the first place, let me tell you now, you need to re-think, why are you setting yourself a goal then? Don't fail before you've already begun.

OK now, we've got that bit straight, here are my top tips in summary to take away from this book that you can quickly refer to when in need:

Here are my top tips that worked for me throughout my weight loss journey and how I managed to succeed, and you can too, applying them to your own goals:

1. Try to pick just 1–2 things you really want to achieve –Don't make it too generic or stereotypical—for example with wanting to 'lose weight', write down what else that goal means to you; what's it really worth to you? Maybe it will make you healthier and fitter, or able to run further, be less lethargic, or perhaps fit in to a dream wedding dress for example?

2. Plan for success – Be methodical and set out exactly how you are going to go about this individual goal. Set measures along the way—having small increments along your entire time frame to measure how you are doing is a great idea as keeps you on track ad motivate to keep at it as you see the results coming to life, on the way to your overall goal.

3. Be realistic with your goals – Sometimes setting yourself a smaller goal is more achievable, than setting yourself up to fail if the goal is too unrealistic. Be reasonable with yourself, and set a good time frame to achieve it in. (Remember, it doesn't matter how slow you go, as long as you just keep on going!)

4. Plan small rewards – As you go along your journey, have small rewards to acknowledge how well you are doing and be proud of what you are doing. If your goal is to lose weight or get healthy, try not to make these rewards food or alcohol. Have other incentives like a pamper day, get your nails done, have a massage, or maybe it's to treat yourself to a new handbag or pair of trainers etc…

5. Think of a new good habit to override this old bad habit you are getting rid of! – It's always a good idea to replace the bad habit with something much better suited to this new you, that way you won't automatically slip back in to old habits, but rather be preoccupied with the new task.

6. Make note of why achieving this will make such a difference in your life and how will it help you – For me, it wasn't just about weight loss, it was about getting healthy and being the best version of me. When I started to look beyond just the physical weight, it became more important for me to stay motivated to become my best self—healthier and fitter than I'd ever been.

7. Just got for it – Stop procrastinating, you know exactly how to start! Just like you learnt to walk, put one foot in front of the other—and bob's your uncle you've started!

8. Perseverance – Yes, this is key! It's your desire to keep on using forward with your goal no matter what. Even if you have a bad day, that does not mean it's over and you've given up! Be persistent—get up tomorrow and carry on! Do not stop.

9. Develop and grow our willpower just like a muscle – We were all born with willpower, but strong will power has to be taught and is gained over time, so learn to practise that self-control each day!

10. Be positive and be happy about why you are doing this! – You know in the long run you will be so happy that you got there in the end, rather than the feeling of giving up and looking back at the time you could have spent keeping on track. Time is going to pass anyway, so don't waste it! Really believe in yourself, you can do it!

11. Enlist the support of those around you! – Make sure your friends and family and even co-workers know that you are doing this, are 110% committed and they should be encouraging you. It can often be hard in the work place, colleagues eating rubbish or going out for cigarette breaks when you have chosen to give these things up. Surround yourself with people that support you, not encourage you to 'just have one'…

12. Feed your ambition and starve your fear – Keep up that visualisation of what achieving this goal means to you, and seek out that inner belief and self-motivation! Stay attentive and focused!

13. Make sure you are in charge of your goals and driving it forward – You can't rely on someone else to make you work out or eat well, at the end of the day, you really are the one to answer to! Don't give up on you and what's important for short-term cravings.

14. Understand your triggers and pitfalls that have let you down in the past – Anticipate the hurdles, know your weaknesses and find solutions for them in advance.

15. Don't beat yourself up if you have a bad day – It's OK, we are all human, acknowledge it happened, sometimes, we do fall down, but it's how quickly you get back up that really counts! Don't get so down about it that you give up—giving up is not an option.

16. LOVE YOURSELF! – Yes, last but not definitely not least, love your god damn self and love the journey! This is your life and time of transition, a period to really get to know yourself and everything you can do. So, enjoy it, it's going to be the best thing you've ever done, trust me! Liberate your life, body and soul!

Along with health and fitness resolutions, you may have other goals you want to achieve, like getting a new job, saving for your dream home, doing a round the world trip, learning to speak another language—but whatever it is, apply these methods, and be one of the statistics that can look back in 4, 8, 12 months and be proud you got what you wanted!

My Goals and Commitments
to Myself

My number #1 goal:

What this really goal means to me:

Realistic timeframe to achieve this:

Incremental measuring points along the way to the overall goal and timeframe:

Small rewards and things to look forward to at the measuring points to acknowledge how well I'm doing:

1.
2.
3.
4.
5.

Final reward to myself when I reach my goal: e.g. new item of clothing, significant event or celebratory activity:

How do I want to feel at that point of reaching my goal?

Summary Once You Reach the Goals

Five things you love about the new you:

1.
2.
3.
4.
5.

Three things you can now do because of these achievements and the qualities you gained from achieving your overall goal:

1.
2.
3.

What one or two things would you like to achieve next with the new you:

1.
2.

My Weekly Calorie Count for Average Eating Amount

MONDAY
A.M.

P.M.

Sub Total

TUESDAY
A.M.

P.M.

Sub Total

WEDNESDAY
A.M.

P.M.

Sub Total

THURSDAY
A.M.

P.M.

Sub Total

FRIDAY
A.M.

P.M.

Sub Total

SATURDAY
A.M.

P.M.

Sub Total

SUNDAY
A.M.

P.M.

Sub Total

Weekly Current Total—
Daily Current Average—

Rpm Calculation—
Rpm + Daily Exercise Calculation—

Calculation of New Daily Average
I Need to Eat Well and Lose Weight—

A Guide to Food Swaps

These were some of the food swaps I started with after figuring out my daily food intake was over 4,000 calories and where I could make some easy first changes to get that reduced to a more appropriate intake:

- White potato to sweet potato
- White rice or brown rice
- White pastas to brown, spinach or pea based pastas, or spiralled veg
- White bread to brown, seeded or rye
- Packaged cereals to porridge and oats
- Hot chips and wedges to sweet potato or roasted vegetables
- Fruit juice to actually eating a piece of fruit instead
- Desserts to yogurt with berries and cinnamon
- Full fat ice cream to healthier versions or yogurt with a dash of maple syrup and nuts
- Biscuits to nuts and dark chocolate
- Cheese and crackers to hummus and vegetable sticks
- Lollies and sweets to frozen grapes or no-sugar jelly, mandarins and raspberries
- Sodas, juices or Frappuccinos to herbal teas and lemon water
- Store brought pizzas and burgers to making my own
- Pasta sauces in a jar to creating my own with no sugar
- Meat containing high fat content to leaner cuts and turkey
- Big bowls of pasta, stir fries or chips to having half the portions as sale instead
- Full breakfast fry up to one with turkey bacon, vegetarian sausages, spinach, tomatoes and eggs
- Cakes, brownies and cupcakes to making your own with half the sugar and fat, or try finding shops that sell vegan options as they are better for you
- Full fat double whipping cream to using coconut milk (canned) to whip in stead
  McDonalds, KFC, Subway etc…try making your own meals at home that will fill you up so you're not grabbing foods like this on the go when needing a quick meal. E.g. wraps, chicken salads, homemade burger patties etc
- Crisps or packets of chips to nuts, vegetable sticks, soya crisps, rice cakes

This should start you off, getting rid of some items you don't need and have more out of habit. It will make you realise that you can still enjoy some of the food you love but that there are in-fact better options for you

(*And never go grocery shopping when you're hungry!)

Bad Cravings and What Your Body Actually Wants

When I'm having an incredibly bad craving and really wanting to be good, as I've mentioned, I always try to talk away, have a moment to myself, breath and have a massive glass of water as often as 9 times out of 10 we are thirsty. (Although I know there are those times where cravings are so intense we just can't think about anything else.)

A lot of cravings and food choices can come from brain chemicals and our thoughts driving our moods and obsessions with certain individual foods like a piece of chocolate or food groups like refined carbs and cakes. But sometimes, our bodies are actually wanting something else, but we override it with emotional food links and habits rather than what we may need.

Then try to combat emotional eating of what I'm craving versus what my body actually needs, and I hope this may help you do the same, as these are same of things that are commonly craved by taste buds, but in actual fact, what we may need more of in our bodies, and this is it's way of trying to tell us so:

Salts—e.g. Chips, crisps, fries, wedges.

Our body is looking for more minerals so try eating more seeds, nuts and fish regularly.

Sugar drinks—e.g. sodas, fruit juices.

Here, we are calling out for calcium, so try getting more dairy, broccoli, seeds, leafy greens, beans or lentils in your diet.

Chocolate—no e.g. necessary for this one LOL!

Our bodies are screaming out for magnesium so try getting more quinoa, cashews, spinach, almonds, tofu and black beans on a regular basis.

Cheese—e.g. apart from the obvious, craving blocks of any cheese, this could also be pizza. Our bodies could be lacking in essential fatty acids so we need to incorporate more Omega-3s in to our daily food intakes. Such as Mackerel, Salmon, walnuts, herring, chia seeds, flax or hemp seeds and egg yolks.

Meats – e.g. steaks, lamb and burgers

Can be linked to a lack of iron, so if you are trying to cut down on big fatty burgers, you can always opt for leaner meat like turkey, or if trying to cut down on that all together try getting more pulses and beans, dried fruit, whole grains, nuts, pumpkin seeds, spinach, eggs or tofu

Refined Carbohydrates (savoury or sweet) as well as lollies and Confectionary – e.g. breads, pastries, muffins, lollies, candy etc…

In general, we can crave these out of boredom and habit, or it could be from a lack of energy to do with our blood sugar levels. Try not to reach for the obvious, instead try subtitled with fresh fruits like potassium rich bananas for a sweet fix and energy, or apples, carrots, pears, grapes or berries, as well as a bowl of porridge with cinnamon or baked sweet potatoes.

These are just a few of the things I've tried, as well as keeping flavoured teas at the ready to have in between meals to curb those cravings that purely come from boredom or could actually be thirst not hunger, so always carry water with you too!

I hope this has all helped in some way to start you on your journey, keep you going through out with any problem, issue or struggle, and get you to where you want to be! Because you will get there if you really want to!

****